BIRD OF THE WEEK

Bird of the Week

JIM FLEGG

Illustrated by Robert Gillmor

BRITISH BROADCASTING CORPORATION

The Radio 4 series Bird of the Week *presented by Jim Flegg was first broadcast in 1980 and 1981. It was produced by John Harrison, of the BBC's Natural History Unit.*

Published by the
British Broadcasting Corporation
35 Marylebone High Street
London W1M 4AA

ISBN 0 563 17950 3
First published 1981
© Jim Flegg 1981

Printed in England
by Mackays of Chatham Ltd

CONTENTS

INTRODUCTION

So many and varied are British birds that all of us have ample opportunity to watch them. They occur in environments of all types – from remote mountain tops to the hearts of our cities, from sun-baked summer holiday beaches to the gloomy depths of conifer woodland in winter. Many frequent our gardens, giving the extra privilege of allowing us to take advantage of their confiding nature and watch them go about their daily business at the bird table or nestbox.

Like a kaleidoscope, they change with the seasons. Spring brings songsters like the Swallow and Nightingale back from Africa, and in autumn, these are replaced by the equally thrilling, but visually more spectacular, wild geese and swans from the Arctic.

Watching, marvelling at the beauty of plumage or listening to the variety of songs, leads on to other things. In one direction, birds can be seen in an artistic sense as just part of a wider landscape: the Skylark an essential element of the summer sky, or ducks flighting across the estuary mudflats in winter. In another, just watching birds leads to a deeper need to know more: about their behaviour, their nests, or about the spectacular feats of endurance and navigation that they perform on their enormous migratory journeys.

Bird of the Week is based on two series of programmes on BBC Radio 4, designed to introduce listeners to the songs of many common (and a few not-so-common) birds, giving a thumbnail sketch of the more fascinating aspects of the life-style of each. These ecological and behavioural cameos have been collected and arranged in a sequence that fits them, broadly speaking, into each week of the calendar year. We start with the Wren in January – almost the smallest of our birds but one of the noisiest – and, not surprisingly, finish with the Robin – so familiar on Christmas cards, but why? – in late December.

Such is the progress of wild birdsong recording that several sets of discs or cassettes of high quality are readily available for those who wish to augment the written word. What was not possible in the radio programmes, but is here, is pictorial illustration. Robert Gillmor has embellished the text with a line drawing, in character, for each *Bird of the Week*.

WREN

Although almost the smallest of British birds (only the Goldcrest and Firecrest are smaller) the Wren is surely the most cheerfully vocal of our birds. Given the slightest suggestion of a fine day, winter or summer, and Wrens are in song, their machine-gun-like bursts of tuneful ebullience astonishingly loud for so small a bird. Often, even when the summer dawn chorus is at its peak, careful listening will show that the Wren is one of the prime songsters.

Despite its small size (less than 10cm long and weighing in at about 10gm or three to the ounce), and relatively unglamorous black-barred chestnut plumage, the Wren is deservedly amongst the most popular of our birds. Back in the days before decimal currency and galloping inflation, it featured – tail as always perkily cocked – on the reverse of our smallest coin, the farthing, the only bird to be honoured in this way.

Perhaps this popularity stems from its presence with us year-round, in almost all habitats – even sea cliffs and dense reed beds, as well as farmland, woodland and our gardens. Wrens cheerfully go about their business, unperturbed by our presence nearby, spending a great deal of time busily scurrying and scuffling among the leaves beneath bushes or in the ivy on old walls or trees, seeking out insects and spiders with their needle-fine beaks.

In cold weather, Wrens tend to gather together in sheltered spots to roost overnight. Sometimes these huddles contain amazing numbers, and over sixty were seen to emerge from a nestbox after one cold winter night, a figure putting the boy-scouts-in-phone-box records to shame. Despite these communal roosts, Wrens are very susceptible to the hardships imposed by bad winter weather, and many may die in prolonged snowfall. In the severe winter of 1962/63, an estimated 70–80% of our Wrens perished from cold. That story had a happy ending, as numbers were back to normal in most areas within three years, and since then have continued to grow to the extent that the Wren may now be one of our most numerous, as well as widespread, birds.

Obviously this implies that given the right conditions, Wrens are highly successful breeding birds. The domed nest is compact and well-camouflaged, made of dry leaves and grasses, and usually embedded in a crevice, or deep in ivy, or even in the pocket of a disused gardening jacket in the shed. The entrance hole is to one

side. The male usually constructs several nests, the female eventually chosing one, to which both birds then add a feather lining. There are usually two or three broods, often of six or more young.

Our bird protection laws, strangely enough, owe much to the Wren. The race of Wrens from the remote island of St Kilda, sixty miles out in the Atlantic west of the Hebrides, are distinct from their mainland counterparts, being larger and greyer. Such was the mania for nest and egg collecting in Victorian times that this island race (its total population was only a couple of hundred pairs) was threatened with extinction at the hands of St Kildans, supplying the demands of Victorian gentlefolk. Once the threat was appreciated, conservationists mounted tremendous pressure to give legal protection to the St Kilda Wren, and from this small beginning, and insignificant but noisy bird, arose modern bird protection legislation.

WILD SWANS

Two species of wild swans visit Britain during the winter months. One, the Whooper Swan, matches our familiar Mute Swan in size (but is lighter in weight) and breeds in arctic Russia and in Iceland, and it is usually these Icelandic birds that we see in Britain, most commonly in the west and north. The Bewick's Swan, which also breeds in arctic Russia, is appreciably smaller and more goose-like than the other two, and occurs by suitable lakes and flooded meadows right across Britain. On land or water both wild swans carry their necks very straight, with the head at right-angles (rather like a walking stick), in contrast to the graceful s posture so typical of the Mute Swan.

Despite the implications of its name, the Mute Swan can produce a variety of grunts and hisses, but these are only audible at close range. In contrast, the wild swans have the most wonderful trumpeting calls, audible for miles on a still day. The atmosphere of these spectacular calls set against the empty grandeur of the arctic tundra and lakes where they breed is thrillingly captured by the Finnish composer Sibelius in *The Swan of Tuonela*.

These far-carrying calls have a vital function to perform when, often in deteriorating autumn weather, families of swans gather to migrate south. The overseas journey from Iceland to northern Scotland is about 600 miles — many flying hours even on a swan's powerful wings and at a typical, wind-assisted, speed of about 75 mph. Some of the journey may be made after dark, or in fog, and the calls help to keep the flock together, preventing the inexperienced youngsters from getting lost on the way. They may even travel in cloud, as swans have been spotted on aircraft control radar migrating from Iceland at the staggering height of 26,000 feet: their identity and altitude were confirmed by the pilot of a passing aircraft!

Two of the best-known places for watching wild swans, Bewick's Swans in particular, are the wildfowl nature reserves of the Ouse Washes in Cambridgeshire and the Wildfowl Trust's headquarters at Slimbridge in Gloucestershire. Unlike the orange and black beak of the Mute Swan, both wild swans have bright yellow and black beaks. The pattern of yellow and black varies from bird to bird, but stays constant throughout the bird's life. Sir Peter Scott and his helpers at Slimbridge have used these beak patterns (in much the

same way as police use the individuality of fingerprints) in a detailed study of Bewick's Swans. They have discovered, for example, that although 'divorces' can occur, most pairs remain intact until one or other adult dies. Each year, the parents migrate south with the brood they have raised (recognisably buffy-grey in colour) and often also with the 'teenage' brood of the previous year. These family parties seem to be the backbone of wild swan social life, and right through the winter they will be found incessantly chatting and grunting in a family conversation to keep close together.

BULLFINCH

Most of us would agree that the Bullfinch *is* a beautiful bird, the male scarlet-breasted, grey-backed and black-capped, his cardinal-like garb giving rise to the colloquial German name 'Dompfaff' or 'cathedral priest'. The female is a subtle mixture of suede-browns, but still with the black cap. Both possess a purplish-black tail and strikingly white patch on the rump, so often all that we see as they dart away deep into the bushes.

But let no one doubt the other side of the Bullfinch character. Beneath that black cap is a sharp, slightly hooked beak, rounder in profile than the typical wedge-shaped beak of a finch. It is ideal for nipping off whole buds from trees and shrubs and biting out the core. This process is so lightning-fast that gooseberry buds can be husked and devoured at the staggering rate of thirty a minute!

Since the time of Queen Elizabeth the First, the Bullfinch has had a price on its head. Even in those far-off, poorly-documented days, gardeners and fruit growers were sufficiently incensed by the havoc caused by Bullfinches eating flower buds during the winter (most attacks occur in January and February) for the chroniclers of the time to note that one penny reward was on offer for 'everie Bulfynche or other Byrde that devoureth the blowthe of fruit'.

Many gardeners or fruit growers, surveying the wreckage after Bullfinches have been feeding (the scattered litter is painfully conspicuous on top of snow) see so many bud fragments that they assume that nothing could have been eaten, and that the attack was sheer wanton vandalism. Not a bit of it. The attack is not only technically skilful, but purposeful. Deep in the heart of the bud lies the flower initial – in a pear bud about the size of a pin-head and looking like a miniature cauliflower. Here, not surprisingly, much of the 'goodness' (in nutritional terms) of the bud is concentrated, and it is this that the Bullfinches are sensibly seeking when they discard the residue of the bud.

For all or most of the year, Bullfinches eat a variety of wild natural foods. In summer, they concentrate on the seeds of dandelion, buttercup and many other plants, turning to nettle, and later dock, in autumn. As winter comes, most seeds fall, but dock and bramble remain available. After Christmas, these seeds are supplemented by ash keys until, late in winter, the buds of blackthorn and hawthorn begin to swell to a worthwhile size. Many Bullfinches will

survive perfectly well all their lives on this natural diet, and it seems that only when natural supplies fail will those birds resident close to gardens or orchards turn their attention to cultivated varieties. When they do, they find them such a palatable alternative that the forthcoming summer's fruit crop is almost destroyed.

During the breeding season, the male is rarely far from his female's side, often singing his whispering, wheezy song. This sounds like a gently swinging creaking gate, very different from the more familiar clearly penetrating whistle that they use to keep in contact with one another in dense undergrowth. They collect food together, often far from the nest, carrying it back in hamster-like cheek pouches to feed the brood on the flat, fragile and twiggy nest, built just like a miniature Woodpigeon's, but deep in the prickly shelter of hawthorn, gorse or bramble.

WIGEON

Artists have long gloried in painting sailing barges against the estuary skyscape, and indeed there are few visions more serene than an estuary on a fine winter's day. The flat landscape rests under a huge upturned bowl of sky. The works of man, be they boats, or farms, or even the far-from-beautiful oil refineries that seem to scar most or our estuaries, are reduced in scale, miniaturised to their proper place. What is the reason for this serenity?

Estuaries, by their very nature, are shallow river mouths, sheltered from wave action, where land water meets sea in a maze of creeks and saltings. Both river and sea contain dissolved nutrients, and these riches mix in the calm waters, resulting in an area of extraordinary nutritional value, capable of supporting teeming invertebrate life, with myriad worms, crustaceans and molluscs; and a wealth of plants, particularly seaweeds but including one or two specialist higher plants like the eel-grass beloved as staple diet by Wigeon.

The Wigeon in one of the most elegant of our wildfowl, trim in silhouette, fast in flight. The duck is a mixture of distinctive cinnamon browns; the drake spectacularly handsome, with gold crown, chestnut head, pink breast and finely vermiculated grey flanks. In flight, he shows a conspicuous large white oval patch on each wing.

Wigeon are dabbling ducks: only rarely will they dive for food, preferring to 'up-end' in the shallows to reach the eel-grass and so-called sea-lettuce. At high tide, when the mudflats are covered and food is out of reach, the Wigeon (unlike most other ducks) turn to another favourite food, short grass. Often the marshes beside the estuary will be used as rough grazing, and those kept close-cropped by sheep are ideal for Wigeon.

Only a few pairs of Wigeon breed in Britain, mostly in Scotland. The majority breed on Arctic tundra. Our winter visiting flocks, often thousands strong, come from as far afield as Arctic Russia, a journey of more than 2000 miles. These migrants often pause in autumn beside the Baltic, or on the extensive estuaries (like the Waddensee) of the Netherlands, until forced to move on as a general freeze – or heavy snowfall – makes their food hard to obtain. Thus both the time of arrival and the numbers of Wigeon wintering in Britain and Ireland are variable. Depending on the severity of the winter elsewhere, in mid-winter we may have more than half of the

Wigeon in Europe.

Once flocks of Wigeon are about, they draw attention to themselves by the clear piercing whistles that the drakes use instead of quacks. These whistles are as mysterious and remote, and as far-carrying, as a bell-buoy on a foggy day when the birds are invisible. On a fine day they are often the prelude to a spectacular fly-past as, with a rush of wings, the Wigeon escape the flooding tide and flight from the estuary to nearby fields.

ROOK

Any fine day from mid-winter onwards, but preferably one with a fresh breeze, Rooks will be seen over or near their rookery, throwing themselves about in the sky in an aerobatic spectacular. Although much of this aerial cavorting may be linked with display and pair formation for the coming breeding season, or with learning and developing vital flying skills, with Rooks (and other members of the crow family) it is difficult to be certain that there is not some element of sheer enjoyment involved, so recklessly enthusiastic do they seem and so pointless otherwise their manoeuvres.

An old adage would suggest that Rooks and the slightly larger but otherwise similar Carrion Crow can be separated on the basis that one on its own will be a Crow, a flock together will be Rooks. This is only broadly true, and a closer inspection is needed to be certain. The Carrion Crow is all-dark, matching its evil reputation, while the feathers of the Rook have a superb purple iridescence when seen well. Crows have a dark beak and a pronounced 'roman nose', while Rooks have a straight-edged pale dagger-like beak, ending (in the adults) in conspicuous pale cheek patches. These are whitish, featherless skin, and expand (like a hamster's cheek pouches) to carry food back to the young in the nest. A final distinguishing feature: Rooks have a conspicuously 'baggy trousered' appearance to their leg feathers, while Carrion Crows seem to be wearing tight-fitting stockings on the upper part of their legs.

The Rookery itself is a township in the sky, with its own complex community structure, and, like modern human communities, with its social problems. The older birds nest in safer, centrally situated sites, in bulky nests created over several years. Newcomers are relegated to the fringes of the colony. Birds are aggressively possessive of their site, and of their nest material, but the minute a back is turned, petty thieving of twigs occurs, ensuring that the rookery is in perpetual turmoil and a cacophony of noise.

Usually the nests are in the tallest trees around. In some areas conifers, oak, ash or beech are used, but over much of lowland England rookeries and spinneys or hedgerows of elms are always associated one with the other. Another old adage, about Rooks deserting dead or dying trees, has more than a grain of truth in it. The recent outbreak of dutch elm disease, which has drastically amended many English farmscapes as trees fall or are felled, has

also caused a great deal of local movement of rookeries, and resulted in some appreciable decreases in Rook numbers.

As the season progresses, so the noise level in the rookery rises. Breeding is early, and the hatching of the young is coincident with spring warmth and moist soils, allowing the Rooks easy feeding. Regrettably, Rooks enjoy freshly sown grain or peas, but any damage they cause is alleviated by the numbers of damaging soil pests like leatherjackets that they consume.

TAWNY OWL

Owls have long fascinated man – perhaps frightened him too. No wizard worth his salt would be without one, and from ancient Egypt and Greek mythology down to Winnie the Pooh, owls have been associated with wisdom.

The Tawny Owl is a comfortable-looking bird, dumpy bodied and round headed, and usually a mixture of browns and chestnuts as its alternative name, Brown Owl, suggests. It is the most widespread and the most numerous of British Owls, and well-liked. We encounter Tawnies more often than the other owls, despite their nocturnal habits, partly because their quavering hooting is so obvious and so exciting, and partly because they have adapted well to co-existence with man. Although primarily birds of mature woodland, they penetrate into the gardens of suburbia and even into the heart of cities like London – anywhere with parks and trees and a supply of mice and sparrows for food.

Owls start their breeding season early. Shakespeare, in *Love's Labour's Lost*, said very appropriately

> 'When icicles hang by the wall,
> And Dick the shepherd blows his nail,
> And Tom bears logs into the hall,
> And milk comes frozen home in pail,
> When blood is nipped and ways be foul,
> Then nightly sings the staring owl —
> Tu who;
> Tu wit tu whoo, a merry note . . .'

Hooting may start before Christmas, and often reaches a crescendo in February as the final squabbles over territorial boundaries are settled. The nest will be in a hollow tree or deserted building: remember Gray's *Elegy:* '. . . yonder ivy-mantled tower, the moping owl doth to the moon complain . . .'

They seem able to gauge the availability of food in the coming summer (mostly small rodents of one sort or another, but including worms, birds, fish and frogs) with accuracy, and lay an appropriate number of eggs. None, or just one or two, if food is scarce, but up to ten if it is plentiful. The female starts incubating as soon as the first egg is laid, so (unlike most birds) the young hatch at intervals of roughly two days. In consequence there is a considerable size dis-

parity between the oldest and the youngest chick: should the owls suddenly fall on hard times, the largest will eat the smallest, then the next smallest . . . Although apparently savage cannibalism, this behaviour does give the family the best chance of producing one or two healthy chicks, rather than *all* the young perishing from starvation.

Owls hunt on silent wings. Their feathers have a velvety surface and the leading edge of the wing a comb-like fringe so that they do not swish through the air as they swoop with outstretched talons on to their prey. An alternative technique is to sit quietly in a tree, feathers blending in good camouflage with the trunk, and wait for the next meal to scamper along the ground below. The attack is then vertical, with wings held cupped like a parachute.

MISTLE THRUSH

The Mistle (or in the past, Missel) Thrush is the largest of our thrushes – a super-size Song Thrush, greyer in colour and with a much longer tail with white edges. In flight, the Mistle Thrush shows conspicuous white underwings (in contrast to the pale chestnut of the Song Thrush) which are made even more obvious by its slow wingbeats, a couple of flaps and then a pause.

It enjoys a special popularity amongst country-lovers as one of the earliest of songsters, and one of the most effective as a soloist. Warm days after the New Year will see all the local males high in the treetops proclaiming territorial boundaries, and the Mistle Thrush habit of continuing to sing in the teeth of the roughest of early spring gales has earned it the nickname 'storm cock'. The song is pure and simple – giving the impression that each note is carefully considered before production to make certain of best effect. It is melodious, and more akin to the Blackbird than to the repetitious phrases of the Song Thrush.

Mistle Thrushes nest very early – often in March. The nest is a large, untidy construction in the fork of a major tree branch, built of grass and just about anything else that is handy. Mistle Thrushes were among the first birds to exploit waste polythene sheet as a nesting material, and a pair in my own garden used streamers of supermarket price labels, several feet long. Such nests are obviously very conspicuous, especially early in the season, and Mistle Thrushes rely on aggression to compensate for this.

The Welsh name – Penn-y-Llwyn – meaning 'master of the copse', is an indication of this renowned aggression. Magpies, Jays and Crows, although larger than the Mistle Thrush, are everyday targets, and even a Buzzard will be treated to their wrath if it comes too near the nest. Marauding cats and foxes are vigorously, and noisily, dive-bombed, and Mistle Thrushes are usually among the first to raise the woodland alarm when a roosting owl is discovered. Although the attack is not often pressed home as far as physical contact, the fuss is usually sufficient to distract the intruder or drive it away.

As their name suggests, Mistle Thrushes are particularly partial to mistletoe berries. Aristotle was aware of this liking, and his name for them – *viscivorus* – is derived from the scientific name for the mistletoe (*Viscum*) and means mistletoe-eater. His epithet is

retained in the scientific name for the Mistle Thrush itself, *Turdus viscivorus*. Although basically woodland birds, they feed much further out in open fields in summer than do Song Thrushes, and the young are specially conspicuous in their pale scaly plumage. In winter, many other berries feature in their diet – even yew, where the poisonous pips pass through undigested. They are often very fond of fallen apples at the stage of alcoholic over-ripeness nearing intoxication!

RAVEN

Over much of Britain and Ireland, we regard the Raven as a bird of mountain and moorland or remote and unpopulated coasts. This distribution is very much a man-made one, and not the Ravens' habitat preference. Before intensive persecution by shepherds and gamekeepers during the nineteenth century, the Raven was widespread even in the lowlands. Modern studies have shown that its evil reputation as a lamb-killer is largely unjustified. In hill country, lambing is hazardous, and weakly or still-born lambs commonplace. Almost always, it is these dead or dying lambs that are 'attacked', as the Raven is a scavenger, not a bird of prey.

This scavenging habit, associated with sheep, is responsible for the Raven's extraordinary early breeding season. Apart from the carrion provided by sheep, hares or deer killed by severe wintry conditions, the major food for the young is the placenta (or afterbirth) from the hill sheep at lambing. Lambing is early in the hills, hence often in February but almost always by March, the Ravens will have eggs. High in the mountains the female will regularly have to sit through blizzard conditions without budging, as even momentary exposure would kill the eggs. By June, the young will be well on the wing, but still moving around in family groups.

Ravens often have enormous territories. In remote areas, ten square miles or more may be needed to provide adequate food. Within this will be several nest sites, and a different one may be used each year. Some sites are ancestral, having been used for decades, sometimes centuries, by succeeding generations. In these cases the nest is really bulky, as each year more branches and fresh greenery are added to it. Some nests are in trees, but probably the majority are well-protected and inaccessible on rocky crags. In 'off' years such nests may be 'borrowed' by a pair of Peregrine Falcons.

The Raven pair during the breeding season will be vociferously aggressive to neighbouring Kestrels, Peregrines or even Golden Eagles, but they seem to take special delight in mobbing Buzzards. Their broad, finger-tipped wings and long, wedge-shaped tail give them good flight control, and they swoop and dive all round the intruder. Buzzards are no mean fliers themselves, and can easily dodge the attacks: often it is difficult to dismiss the thought that the birds are all enjoying their mastery of the air and just playing.

These aerobatic skills are brought out to the full during courtship

display. The pair will roll and tumble in the air, occasionally lock-
ing their talons belly-to-belly and falling head-over-heels for hundreds of feet before pulling up in a feather-tearing turn. All of this is
accompanied by the Raven's gruff honking croak – an unmistakable
noise echoing off the surrounding crags and very much one of *the*
sounds of the mountains.

SISKIN

Siskins, one of the smallest of our finches, do breed in this country but the population is augmented in winter by migrant birds from Scandinavia. Their natural winter habitat is first among stands of silver birch and later in the tops of the alder trees lining the banks of rivers and streams. In winter they are dark grey-green enlivened with yellowish wingbars and a pale yellow-buff belly. They feed (often in company with Redpolls) on the seeds within the alder cones. These, like miniature wooden pineapples, are carried in clusters at the extreme tips of the flimsy branches, and to reach them the Blue-tit-sized Siskin must use all the nimble agility, and ability to hang upside-down, that we usually associate with tits.

In those parts of England where orchards occur, Siskins have, during the last decade, been presented by man with an opportunity for expansion. Most modern orchards are protected by planted windbreaks: poplars and conifers enjoyed brief popularity, but soon demonstrated disadvantages and were replaced very largely with several species of alder, which thrive despite the absence of a watercourse. These are now mature enough to bear cones, and over much of southern England the Siskin is now an everyday bird of orchards in winter.

It would seem that Siskins are not only quick to exploit new feeding opportunities provided by man, but that they learn and 'spread the message' quickly. In the early 1960s, birdwatchers started to use plastic net bags full of peanuts to attract birds to their gardens. The tits, of course, were expected as visitors, but Siskins soon also discovered this welcome food supply. Now there are few areas where Siskins cannot be expected to visit peanut bags in reasonably-sized suburban or rural gardens. They have a strongly-marked preference for orange plastic – perhaps because this is visible at long range.

Siskins tend to visit nut bags relatively late in the season, late in February or during March. Probably they use the very rich food content of the nuts to build up body fat as a 'fuel' reserve for migration back to their Scandinavian breeding forests, or if they are part of the expanding British breeding population, to get into good condition for the fast-oncoming breeding season. Large expanses of conifers seem to be a necessity for breeding colonies, particularly in Scotland and Ireland, but increasingly now further south as

commercial reafforestation areas mature. The neat nest is situated high up in the tree and well out on a horizontal branch: often the best indication that breeding birds are present is the song – a musical twittering often ending in a broad, nasal 'zwee'.

At close range on the nut bag, the Siskins' full beauty can be enjoyed. As the breeding season approaches, so the elegant male becomes more golden yellow below, with a yellow neck and face offset by black crown and bib. Although several may feed together they are aggressive and uneasy neighbours. Threat displays are common – when the neat, deeply forked, dark tail is suddenly fanned to expose the bright yellow patches at its base, the wings are half spread to show the golden wingbars more boldly, and the aggressor lunges forward with beak half-open to intimidate his rival, making a colourful spectacle.

DUNNOCK

The Dunnock is often called the Hedge Sparrow, but misleadingly, as although 'hedge' is appropriate, a closer view will show a needle-fine, insect-eating beak very different from the squat, seed-crushing wedge-shaped beak of the House Sparrow, to which the Dunnock in not related. The name derives from the Old English 'dun' – an indeterminate sort of brown – and 'ock', meaning little. Dun is a harsh description of the Dunnock's plumage: breast, throat and face are an unusual leaden grey, while the back is a mixture of browns, chestnut and black.

This tweed-like mixture comes into its own during the breeding season. Dunnocks build neat grass and moss nests, hair lined, usually low in brambles, shrubs or hedges. Before the bushes leaf out, camouflage is at a premium, and few birds are less visible, crouched low in a nest of old brown grass, than the hen Dunnock. She sits very tight, no twitch of tail or flicker of eyelid betraying her position. Once disturbed, though, the clutch of eggs her departure reveals seem the antithesis of camouflage, as they are bright blue, unspeckled, and stand out glaringly against their sombre background.

Another colloquial name – Hedge Betty – gives an indication of the endearing nature of Dunnocks. They seem always active, even fussy in their feeding as they hop along deep under the bushes picking up such minute food items that even binoculars cannot help to identify. Rarely do they seem flustered by nearby humans, and go about their business as if we did not exist. In spring, the gardener may find himself in the centre as male dances round female, wings and tail flicking almost in a frenzy, and there will be short, excited chases, punctuated by bursts of song. This is tuneful and cheerful, if slightly scratchy, and ends in mid-stream, almost as it were with a question mark.

Question mark is appropriate, for despite the opportunity for close observation we still know surprisingly little about this enigmatic bird. Its social behaviour and diet are poorly understood, as is the reason for the occasional evening chorus of shrill, piping Dunnock alarm calls when no predators are about. Sometimes a woodland on a summer evening will appear *full* of Dunnocks – each only a few yards from its neighbour, and each piping loudly. Most of our Dunnocks are decidedly stay-at-home: ringing recoveries indicate a sedentary existence. But every few years, there is evidence of

considerable autumn migration, and large numbers of Dunnocks appear at coastal bird observatories. Why? And why should this tame and approachable garden bird in Britain be translated into an extremely shy denizen of deepest cover, rarely seen, on the Continent, even in those countries where small-bird persecution is not the rule?

SONG THRUSH

'. . . That's the wise thrush; he sings each song twice over,
Lest you should think he never could recapture
The first fine careless rapture!'

So wrote Robert Browning in *Home thoughts from abroad*. Although the Song Thrush is rarely as precise as Browning suggests, the repetition of simple, fluting song phrases two or three times in succession is the key to identifying Song Thrush song. It clearly sets the Song Thrush apart from the extended and more melodious phrases of the Blackbird in the woodland or garden dawn and dusk choruses. This rather stereotyped performance might not appear to lend itself to mimicry, but Song Thrushes are masters at imitating telephone bells – much to the gardener's annoyance.

Song Thrushes are confidingly present in the garden year-round, and often come as close to the fork as a Robin. In winter, numbers are augmented by wilder birds from the north, which are often to be seen dotted across damp meadows, coming closer to man only during the severest weather.

From January in warmer winters, the males stake claim to territory, singing from a number of prominent perches around its margins. In mild years, the first nests appear in March, often painfully conspicuous in hedgerows or garden shrubs before they leaf out. The nest is very characteristic, with four to six sky-blue eggs, coarsely peppered with a few large black spots. These nestle safely in a neatly woven grass basket, lined (astonishingly) with mud, smoothly finished after an exceedingly neat plastering job. The stubby-tailed youngsters, once past the naked and helpless stage, are noisy miniatures of their parents, squawking demandingly for a never-ending supply of worms.

Later in the summer, when dry soils make worm-finding more difficult, the Song Thrush exploits a surprisingly unusual food source for birds – snails. Song Thrushes have developed the technique of smashing open snail shells, often choosing a particular section of the garden path. In the country, they will chose a suitable large stone, and use this as an 'anvil' on which to hammer the shell apart. These anvils are easily recognised on woodland paths by the multicoloured litter of snail shell fragments surrounding them.

Song Thrushes are smaller and more upright in stance than

Blackbirds or Mistle Thrushes, and are often bullied into yielding worms to these larger relatives. During the winter, worms (and other small soil animals) and berries are taken with equal freedom. Hawthorn hedges or rowan trees rich and colourful with berries are ideal places to seek close-up views of Song Thrushes in action.

CHAFFINCH

Chaffinches make an early start to the singing year. From February onwards their boisterous song – a long descending trill with a final characteristic swashbuckling flourish – can be heard just about anywhere you go. The Chaffinch is a serious contender (with the Blackbird) for the title of 'most numerous British bird' with a recent estimate of about seven million breeding pairs. In winter, the numbers of both species are augmented by migrants, and probably then the Chaffinch may win by a whisker!

In winter, many Chaffinches desert woodland and join with other finches and buntings – and the ubiquitous House Sparrow – in mixed feeding flocks on stubble, weedy fields or rough ground. Both on the ground and in the air at this time the common call is a strident 'pink pink' – no wonder the Dutch call the Chaffinch 'Fink'. This same 'pink' call is the basis for summer alarm calls, often generated by the discovery of a Tawny Owl trying to snooze through the daylight hours in peace and quiet.

The plumage is as unmistakable as the song, the male handsome with deep pink breast, dove grey head (with a black top-knot) and bold white wingbars on dark wings. In winter, he is rather drabber, more like the female and well-camouflaged in dead grass and stubble. She retains this beige mixture through the summer too, to camouflage her on the nest.

Not just the female, but the nest also is well-camouflaged. Usually it is set in a crotch close against a lichen-covered trunk, and the whole is one of the neatest nests made by any bird. The basic cup is made of fine grasses and moss, and lined with hair. The exterior is a marvel of concealment, for pieces of lichen are woven into the structure in a very lifelike, flaky fashion, so that it is difficult to be certain where tree ends and nest begins. This is important, as nesting starts early, often before leaves provide shelter from prying eyes.

One of the marvels of bird song is how such complicated and beautiful melodies are passed on from generation to generation. Are the songs learnt, son listening to father? Or does some genetic wizardry ensure that the egg contains a chick ready-programmed to delight us next spring? Research workers at Cambridge University have unravelled this mystery, at least for the Chaffinch. The basic framework of the song seems to be inherited, and will be produced

automatically, even by a young Chaffinch raised in total isolation from others of its kind. In the wild, the young male, possessing this instinctive foundation, will listen to his elders and gradually develop the trills and flourishes of his full song. In this way, too, local 'dialects' develop, making (for example) West Country Chaffinches sound as different as their human counterparts to a visitor from, say, the south-east.

HOUSE SPARROW

The House Sparrow must surely be the most familiar of British birds. 'Familiar' is an appropriate word, too, because House Sparrow always seem to be in close association with man and his buildings. In the hills, or on open marsh or moor, they are not to be seen, but as soon as you reach a cluster of occupied farm buildings, and the shelter and food that they provide, then a colony of House Sparrows is inevitably present.

Those of us who travel about Britain will have noticed how much brighter is the plumage of Sparrows away from industrial areas. There was recently some debate over whether Sparrows were actually evolving a darker plumage – called 'industrial melanism' – as have some moths, or just getting contaminated with soot and dirt. The latter turned out to be the case!

With such a close association with man, it is hardly surprising that House Sparrows are common bird-table visitors, eating just about anything. Watch the eagles and vultures being fed in the Zoo, and be amazed (and perhaps slightly worried in the light of the Alfred Hitchcock film *Birds*) when the Sparrows nip in quick and set about the meat before its rightful owners wake up! Other Sparrows have decided that *outdoor* life is no longer necessary: many main line stations have indoor populations, as do grain stores and large factories. The apparent lack of food in the last is more than compensated for in offerings from the sandwich lunches of the human workforce.

The 'song' of a territory-holding male House Sparrow is such a monotonous chirrup that it is tempting to say 'only another Sparrow could fall for that' – but that, after all, is its purpose. Sparrows can breed at almost any time of the year, so that chirrup is a familiar noise, as is the sight of the drabber female, a streaky mixture of buffs and browns, perching on the guttering with wings shivering. Displays often seem to get more and more excited, even out of hand, resulting in furious chases and rough-and-tumbles between males and females.

Our Sparrows are representatives of the tropical weaverbird family, some of which, in Africa, are as devastating pests to cereal crops as are plagues of locusts. No wonder, then, that our Sparrows flock into the corn at harvest time, doing considerable damage. Most gardeners are more annoyed by the apparent vandalism of House

Sparrow: we put food out for them, they eat it, and then start to tear up the crocuses and primulas. Although this may seem to be hooliganism, it is not so. Notice how often it is *yellow* flowers that are attacked. Yellow colouration is associated with a rich supply of nectar – yellow crocuses have far more than purple ones – and it is this nectar at the base of the flower that the House Sparrows are after.

At the end of the day, Sparrows gather in large communal roosts, under the eaves or in dense clumps of rhododendrons or ivy-clad trees. Here their squabbling chatter persists until long after dark.

BLACKBIRD

The *Atlas of Breeding Birds in Britain and Ireland* suggests that not only is the Blackbird one of the most widespread of our breeding birds, it is also one of the most numerous, recorded over 96% of the land surface and with a breeding population estimated at seven million pairs. As the Blackbird has such a beautiful fluting warble of a song – certainly most birdwatchers would rate it among their 'Top Ten' favourites – this very commonness seems to be an added bonus. You would never hear somebody say 'that's just another old Blackbird singing'.

Although the colours of the male are simple in the extreme – rich velvety jet-black feathers, strikingly offset by an orange beak and eye-ring – they can hardly be bettered for elegance. The female seems more homely in her brown feathers – plump, and somehow motherly, with a comfortable-looking speckled pale apron drawn up to her chin. An attractive feature of Blackbirds is the way they live cheerfully and successfully in our towns, even though they seem distressingly often to fall prey to cats, or (under the pressures of dashing about finding worms to feed their youngsters) to hurl themselves fatally in front of cars.

Thus most of us can hear Blackbirds singing, and can observe them as they go about their daily lives near our homes. Most of us must have seen neighbouring males, each puffed up with his own importance to present an intimidating appearance, pacing for hours, sometimes days, along opposite sides of the imaginary line separating their territories.

After a mild winter, Blackbirds get down to nesting early, and in the south chicks may hatch in March. There may often be three broods in a season, and a number of pairs are on record as having nested *five* times – successfully – in one year! With each brood up to five or six nestlings strong, there is obviously a huge infant and juvenile mortality rate – maybe 90% or higher on occasions – otherwise we would be over-run with Blackbirds.

During the autumn, our own birds (which tend not to move very far) are joined by millions of migrants escaping from the snow and ice of northern Europe. At good migration-watching points on the east coast, on some November days it can almost seem to be raining Blackbirds, so fast do they dive from the skies into the clumps of sea buckthorn and hawthorn. These birds feed in our woods and

orchards, gathering together in the evening in huge roosts in dense thickets.

The male does a lot of keeping watch during the breeding season, alert for marauding cats, whose presence he announces with strident alarm calls that alert not only his own family, but everyone else besides. At roosts during the winter, there often seems to be a ritual performance of these 'clucking' and 'pinking' alarm calls before night comes and they all settle down.

WILLOW WARBLER

If ever a songbird deserved to be called 'harbinger of spring' it is the Willow Warbler. The silvery descending trill of song immediately conjures up visions of yellow-green early beech leaves, just bursting from the bud, dappled spring sunshine on primrose banks, and perhaps, too, the sweetness of the smell of woodland carpeted in bluebells.

Unlike the Chiffchaff – a near relative almost impossible to distinguish save by its vastly different, monotonous 'chiff-chaff' song – the Willow Warbler migrates far south to the tropics of Africa for the winter. Most birds moult – to replace worn out feathers – once each year, but not the Willow Warbler. This tiny scrap of birdlife, weighing one third of an ounce, moults twice – once before it goes, and once again in Africa just before it returns. That something so small can successfully endure the enormous double journey beyond the equator and back, *and* find the energy to replace its plumage twice each year, should fill us with wonder. Add to it the pin-point navigational accuracy that the adults achieve in returning to precisely the same patch of woodland in successive years, and you wonder whether mankind is right to glory in his inventions of navigational computers, or even (considering the tiny size of a Willow Warbler brain) in the microchip!

Willow Warblers love scrubby areas like blackthorn and hawthorn thickets, rather than dense woodland of tall trees, which is more the home of the Chiffchaff. In consequence, they have a much wider habitat adaptability than the Chiffchaff, which enables them to penetrate in the silver birch scrub right up to the extreme north of Scotland, while Chiffchaffs become thin on the ground after the Borders.

Even open moorland areas are being made more acceptable to Willow Warblers by reafforestation schemes – the young conifer plantations being ideal habitat. The Willow Warbler seems to be establishing itself as our most numerous and widespread summer migrant, considerably commoner than the Swallow.

The nest is usually very well concealed, more or less on the ground in thick long grass, and with a dome of woven grass stems overhead. In high summer, the adults feed a lot on small insects, often catching them on the wing, or plucking aphids from leaves, hovering almost like hummingbirds while they do. In no way are

they averse to larger prey when an opportunity arises, and Willow Warblers can sometimes be seen on a grassy track struggling to subdue a large green caterpillar seemingly as large as itself. Always appearing busily industrious, Willow Warblers normally manage to raise two broods each summer, sometimes three. Despite this, they also manage to find time to sing between broods, keeping the summer woodland full of their superb song.

GREAT NORTHERN DIVER

Of all the bird calls in the World, that of the Great Northern Diver must rate as one of the most fabulous and thrilling, echoing wildly between the mountains and across the lochs of its breeding grounds. The Americans call divers 'loons', and it is tempting to assume that this name comes from the maniacal laughing in the song. A more likely derivation is from the Icelandic 'lomr' or loom, for lame or clumsy. Great Northern Divers would be familiar birds to Icelanders, who would be well aware of their undoubted clumsiness on land.

In summer, the bird is as spectacular as its song. Goose-sized, with a short neck and powerful dagger-like dark beak, supremely elegant, the black head with a greenish sheen, the black back chequered with brilliant white squares. The earliest diver-like fossils are over a hundred million years old, amongst the earliest of fossil birds, and the continued presence of such a 'primitive' line testifies to divers' success as underwater fishers.

The body is well streamlined, torpedo-shaped with the wings reduced in size. The feet are large, with lobed toes, and set back near the tail for best propulsion – hence their clumsiness on land. Divers only come ashore to struggle the few feet on to their nest, otherwise they spend most of their lives on the water.

The nest is usually beside a large, lonely loch, although the birds may fly out to sea sometimes to feed. In Britain in summer, they are exceedingly rare, with only a handful of breeding records in northern Scotland. The story told by Arthur Ransome in his children's classic *Great Northern* of the threat to these birds from egg-collectors, is sadly all too true, even in the remotest parts of the highlands. More often, we will see Great Northern Divers during the winter, when the plumage is a much drabber variety of greys. Coastal waters, estuaries and, often, large reservoirs well-stocked with fish, are all favoured localities.

Reservoirs offer an excellent chance to watch the fishing technique. The hunting diver will patrol on the surface, often putting its head underwater to scan for fish. If it sights likely prey, it seems to slip under water, just sinking gradually from view leaving hardly a ripple. Once under water, divers are fast swimmers capable of staying submerged for about a minute.

There are, of course, some disadvantages to this degree of special-

isation for fishing. Clumsiness on land is one, not too important perhaps, but another – the small, stiff wings, better underwater than in the air – does pose the diver some flying problems. The Great Northern Diver is a large, heavy bird, and with such small wings needs a long take-off run, pattering across the water for many yards before getting airborne. Landing requires a similarly long runway if the venture is not to end in an undignified splash!

SWIFT

Not so long ago, Swifts were called 'Devil Birds', doubtless because of their unearthly screeching cries and their all-black plumage. During the summer, gangs of Swifts will sweep through the streets in the older parts of the town, flying flat-out and screaming all the time, seeming to risk life and limb in collisions with phone wires and traffic, but in reality well in control of their manoeuvres.

Over the centuries, Swifts must be one of few birds to have *benefited* from the overall spread of urban man. Doubtless in the old days they nested in cracks in cliffs and caves – perhaps even in hollow trees as some species do elsewhere in the world today – but throughout Europe, they are now confirmed city dwellers.

Of all British birds, Swifts are the most aerial. They feed, sleep and even mate on the wing. If they come to ground accidentally, they find it almost impossible to take off again unaided. Those flickering long slender wings indicate a bird designed for speed, as does the streamlined body with eyes recessed like the headlights of a sports car. In level flight, Swifts can easily exceed 60 mph, and we know that they can climb many thousands of feet to roost, catnapping on the wing, or in search of the flying insects that are their sole food. Although the beak looks tiny from outside, it is capable of gaping open literally from ear to ear: an effective flying insect net. We know, too, from studies of their movements by radar, that they can fly hundreds of miles non-stop in search of good feeding – a very necessary ability when you think of the impact of our fickle summer weather on their food insects.

The nest is normally built in a hole under the eaves that can be entered in flight. It is a skimpy affair, as the Swift can only gather the debris in the roof and line it with a few feathers caught in mid-air. Usually there are two or three chicks, which show an amazing tenacity to life. Obviously they are even more vulnerable than their parents to food shortages caused by bad weather, but have developed the ability to lapse into a torpor – a sort of mini-hibernation – until things improve. Their body temperature drops, the pulse slows right down, and growth ceases. In this state, they can survive without food for several days. As a result, the time taken for them to reach fledging size varies from about five weeks in a good summer to two months in a bad one!

Despite their highly specialised and apparently risky life style,

Swifts are highly successful birds. Many may live for ten years or more, unusually long for a small bird. They are migrants, wintering in central Africa: one of the latest to arrive (in mid-May) and earliest to leave, during August. Taking into account their totally aerial life, a rough calculation shows that the oldest Swift on record – which lived to sixteen – must have exceeded 4,000,000 flying miles in its lifetime!

CUCKOO

With its simple call so easy to mimic instrumentally, perhaps it is not surprising that the Cuckoo is popular with composers: the country idyll of Beethoven's Pastoral Symphony, for example, or Delius' *On hearing the first Cuckoo in Spring.* That theme has also stimulated generations of letter-writers to *The Times*, taking part in a 'race' to hear the first Cuckoo each year. Certainly the Cuckoo should not be regarded as a harbinger of spring, as it is such a late migrant: an anonymous thirteenth-century poet had it right when he wrote: 'Sumer is icumen in, lhude sing cuccu!''

The Cuckoo is an amazing bird, its life-cycle an essay in the marvels of evolution. Let us start at the beginning, with the adult female, a bird about the size of a pigeon, returning from Africa. In Britain, most Cuckoos are associated with one to three common foster parents: Reed Warblers in marshland, Meadow Pipits on moorland, and Dunnocks on farmland. Even a Cuckoo laying for the first time will be able to seek out the correct habitat and host, so that the eggs she lays will be close enough imitations to fool the foster parents. She will hunt through her territory, locating appropriate foster nests, laying as soon as they are ready with a part-complete or recently-completed clutch.

Egg laying takes only a moment in a swift visit. The Cuckoo's wings hardly stop beating as she lands on the nest, lays her egg, snatches up a host egg and departs. The Cuckoo egg is specially quick to develop, taking only ten or eleven days, and is usually a couple of days faster than the host. The chick that emerges is a muscular baby and, wriggling beneath its unfortunate foster brothers and sisters (or any remaining eggs), arches its back, braces itself with its embryo wings – and hoists them up and out over the side of the nest, where of course they perish.

Thereafter, the baby Cuckoo grows at a furious pace, soon dwarfing the nest and its foster parents, who must be driven mad by its incessant, but obviously very effective, wheedling cries for food. Even after it has left the nest – by which time the adult Cuckoos have all departed for Africa – the fledgling produces a call that will stop *any* food-carrying parent in its tracks, and draw it (like a powerful magnet) to stuff its beakful into the tempting orange gape of the young Cuckoo. At least one unfortunate Wren is on record as having overdone it by falling into that capacious throat, suffocating both

the Cuckoo and itself!

Then comes the last episode in this amazing story: a month or more after the adults have migrated, the young Cuckoos set off, on their own, with nothing save their instinctive navigation systems to guide them, to the wintering areas in tropical Africa.

Considering the unpleasant connotations of cuckolding, it is surprising that the bird today is so popular. Shakespeare thought otherwise in *Love's Labour's Lost:*

> 'Cuckoo; cuckoo; cuckoo; O word of fear
> Unpleasing to a married ear.'

MEADOW PIPIT

Relatively few birds find the windblown and often wet expanses of moorland an acceptable home, but the Meadow Pipit is perhaps the most characteristic small bird of the mosses, heather, bracken, bog and rough grassland.

For much of the year, pipits seem to spend a lot of time on the ground, running about at high speed snapping up insects. They are small birds, rather like stretched Dunnocks with long athletic legs, and, like the Dunnock, with plumage a tweedy mixture of dark streaks on a brownish or olive background, sometimes quite golden in autumn. This gives excellent camouflage against a peat or dry grass background.

One exception to this earthbound way of life is the display flight, when the male rises steeply fifty feet or more into the air, then slowly descends – wings extended and fluttering rapidly, tail fanned – just like a parachute, producing all the while a cheerfully tinkling, trilling song.

Naturally, in this terrain the nest is on the ground, a deep grass-lined cup tucked away in the base of a tussock and containing four to six dark brown speckled eggs. At this time, we would find the nest very difficult to locate, so cautious are the birds, but not so for the female Cuckoo. Meadow Pipits are probably the commonest hosts of Cuckoos in Britain: certainly in the uplands. In late May and June, female Cuckoos can be seen patrolling the moors, observing Meadow Pipit movements closely and thus locating their nests. As they move about, the Cuckoos cause a great deal of alarm – not surprisingly – and agitated Meadow Pipits follow them about, calling shrilly, sometimes attacking and even causing feathers to fly.

Once the young Meadow Pipits have hatched, although safe from Cuckoos they face many other hazards – weasels, stoats and foxes on the ground, Carrion or Hooded Crows in the air. No wonder the parents have penetrating alarm calls, so piercing that even a Pipit with a beak packed with juicy wriggling caterpillars for its young can warn its family to lie low and say nothing.

Much of moorland Britain in winter is too bleak even for Meadow Pipits, and the birds descend to lower altitudes during the autumn, favouring coastal marshes, riverside meadows and arable farmland. Here they are joined by many European Meadow Pipits seeking refuge from the harsh Continental winter. Some of these, and some

of our own breeding birds, will move further south (particularly to Spain and Portugal) as winter progresses, returning to announce the arrival of spring on the moors with their exultant song.

WHITETHROAT

Early in the summer, particularly when the need to advertise and defend a territory is at its greatest, Whitethroats indulge in song flights, shooting skywards over the bushes to thirty or forty feet. There they hover uncertainly, jerking about, singing a few jaunty, scratchy phrases, before plunging headlong back down into the cover.

The Whitethroat is one of our summer-visitor warblers, tit-sized, and widespread in hedgerows, on rough scrubland and on gorse-covered heaths. Although basically skulking, they seem unable to resist the temptation to peek out at you inquisitively from the depths of cover, churring a cautionary message to their neighbours as they do so.

Though the female is sombre in plumage for effective camouflage on the nest, the male, albeit not gaudy, is really very attractive with conspicuous chestnut wings, pinkish breast, long white-edged tail regularly cocked up and down, grey cap and, of course, a white throat. As he inspects you, tail flicking, so the feathers of his crown are raised and lowered, altering the profile of his head completely. When he does burst into song – and with the Whitethroat, *burst* is an expressive word for the explosive volume he produces, then the white throat feathers are puffed out conspicuously too.

Whitethroats were once one of our commonest summer migrants, but suddenly, in 1969, some calamity struck them, reducing numbers by up to 80% in some areas. Our Whitethroats spend the winter in West Africa, south of the Sahara Desert, in a region of scrubland called the Sahel, where the vegetation is used to, and tolerant of, short periods of drought. It is thought that the drought out there, extending over several years, that caused so much human suffering and loss of cattle, also caught the Whitethroat. Normal numbers left Britain in autumn 1968, but very few returned, and we think that the impact of the drought and, just as important, overgrazing by starving cattle on the vegetation of the Sahel, suddenly proved a bit too much. Whitethroats need a rich food supply for some weeks to fatten-up for their enormous non-stop journey north across the Sahara: it seems likely that most just could not gather enough food and perished in the desert.

Fortunately, nature is always demonstrating her basic robustness, and the sad history of the Whitethroat is no exception: it has a

happier ending. After just over a decade of at first rarity, then scarcity, Whitethroats are happily on the increase again. Although numbers are not yet back to the pre-catastrophe level, none of us on a summer country walk should find it too difficult to locate the scratchy melody of this attractive bird.

NIGHTINGALE

The voice of the Nightingale, heard as a solo at dead of night, comes through the clear warm summer air as one of the most fabulous bird songs in the world. Certainly for most of us it is as near to perfection in British bird song as we are likely to get. Part of the thrill of listening lies in the variety – from throaty chuckles to far-carrying whistles – and part in the tonal range, from rich cello-like phrases to the purest of treble trills.

Milton, in *Paradise Lost*, says

> 'All but the watchful Nightingale
> She all night her amorous descant sung'

This is not quite true: Nightingales sing a great deal during the day too, but tend to get swamped by the variety of other birdsong around. Why they sing so much at night is not fully understood. Few songbirds sing at night, but two that do, the Grasshopper Warbler and the Reed Warbler are birds of dense cover like the Nightingale. Like the Nightingale, they are summer visitors to this country and migrate by night. One theory is that the males migrate some days before the females: on arrival they set up territory, and then sing to the night skies to attract their female as she passes over.

Of course if you live in Nightingale country, basically woodland or extensive scrub and southeast of a line from the Severn to the Humber, this habit of bellowing a song into the midnight air can become obtrusive. The fascinating collective noun for a group of Nightingales is a 'watch', from the same origins as the watch kept by sailors or sentries. Most of us, surely, would prefer to lie awake and listen, glorying in the song.

For such superb songsters, Nightingales are very drab in plumage, a case of 'not being able to have everything'. Between Robin and Song Thrush in size, they are chestnut-brown all over, enlivened only by a long, rich rufous tail. This is often all that you see, as generally Nightingales are shy of coming into the open, preferring to scold intruders from concealment with a surprisingly varied repertoire of chacks and churrs. The nest is a masterpiece of concealment, built of dead leaves and with a grass-lined cup containing four or five very dark olive eggs. Placed close to the ground, deep in nettles or a tangle of bramble, it is practically undetectable.

Their shyness, and this rather gruff treatment of strangers,

detracts not one bit from Nightingales' performance as songsters. They have all the breath and volume control they need to sing magnificently from the deepest cover. At the height of the all-too-short six-week song period in May and June, males will sing against one another to proclaim their territories.

What better place for the Nightingale than this, at the climax of a verse of good wishes in Robert Louis Stevenson's *Underwood:*

> 'Go, little book, and wish to all
> Flowers in the garden, meat in the hall
> A bin of wine, a spice of wit,
> A house with lawns enclosing it,
> A living river at the door
> A nightingale in the sycamore.'

MANX SHEARWATER

Manx Shearwaters are slender-winged seabirds, the size of a small gull, which nest underground mostly on remote and usually uninhabited islands, and which visit their breeding areas only at night. Usually, as dusk falls, the Shearwaters gather in huge 'rafts' offshore. In the north of Britain, and in Scandinavia, there are some mainland colonies, usually relatively small. Normally colonies are on the cliff top, or close to the shore of low-lying islands, but a striking exception is the colony more than a mile from the sea and some two thousand feet up in the rocky screes in the centre of Rum, one of the islands of the Inner Hebrides.

As their name suggests, at sea Shearwaters fly low, often touching the waves with one wing tip as they bank and turn. This characteristic flight, coupled with black-above, white-below plumage, makes them unmistakable. They are masters of energy-conserving flight. The wings are long and narrow, and held stiff, slightly bowed downwards. Only in very still air do they flap: otherwise, Shearwaters cut at speed across the ocean air currents, gaining lift even off the waves, and Welsh birds may regularly fish for food as far away from home as the Bay of Biscay.

By day, walking the cliff top, there would be no reason to suspect that a colony existed in the 'rabbit burrows' all around. At night, the adults' eerie caterwauling as they fly overhead with a rush of air like a wartime shell, gives the game away. The tremendous cacophony of a large colony on the Calf of Man is described in one of the Icelandic *Sagas*, and in Norway in the past, the mysterious and terrifying noises were attributed to angry trolls.

The adults change over incubation duty, or feed their solitary chick, covered in great masses of fluffy grey down, only at night, to escape the savage predation that the Great Black-backed Gull can wreak as the clumsy Shearwaters struggle towards their burrows. The sitting bird may have been waiting a few days for its mate to return from a fishing trip, and responds eagerly to the crowing, cooing call as it passes overhead. In this way, even in the dark, the right nest is quickly located. Their powers of navigation and homing are considerable. Some years ago, a bird removed from her egg in a burrow on Skokholm, Pembroke, was taken by aircraft to Boston, USA, and liberated. She had returned to her burrow before the letter announcing her release had reached the island!

The nest is often in a rabbit burrow – the hapless rabbits are quickly evicted – or in burrows dug by the birds themselves, or in natural holes in rock screes. The parents feed the single youngster a smelly, oily mixture of fish and plankton which is very nutritious. On this it grows quickly, becoming very fat (and itself nutritious: in Australasia, a related species – the 'mutton bird' – is still eaten by man). A couple of weeks before fledging it is far too heavy to fly: its parents then abandon it and return to sea, while it converts its stored fat into muscle and completes its feather growth, eventually slimming and maturing sufficiently to emerge one night from its burrow to embark on its maiden flight, *en route* to wintering grounds off Brazil.

KITTIWAKE

The sound of breaking waves accompanies Kittiwakes all their lives, as much a feature of the stormy ocean where they spend the winter as it is at the foot of their nesting cliffs. The Kittiwake is small and slender for a gull, elegant, silver-backed and with tern-like black-tipped wings. It is pleasantly free from some of the features of its larger relatives (like cannibalistic attacks on the eggs or young of their own, or other, species) which do not endear them to man. Many of the other gulls maintain an association with man through the winter, feeding inland behind the plough or scavenging on refuse tips: not so the Kittiwake, which remains essentially a 'sea' gull.

The Kittiwake, like the Cuckoo, is an excellent example of a bird that, quite clearly and without argument, calls its own name. Raucous cries of 'Kitti-wa-a-a-ke' readily lead the birdwatcher towards the breeding grounds. Kittiwakes build their nests in colonies, often hundreds of pairs strong, usually on sheer cliff faces around the coast or on offshore islands. The cliff chosen may often have a considerable overhang, and a good definition of a Kittiwake nest site would be that no other bird could nest there! The slightest of projecting rocks, even under the overhang, serves as a foundation on which a nesting platform is built. The nest is about a foot in diameter, and made of mud, seaweed and a wide (and often colourful) variety of flotsam and jetsam, all cemented together, and made conspicuous as time goes by, with liberal whitewashings of tacky droppings. In areas lacking suitable cliffs, Kittiwakes readily resort to man-made alternatives, and there are several colonies on piers and sea-front warehouse window-ledges!

Colonial seabirds tend to be rather smelly and pretty noisy. Nests are so close that real fighting could easily dislodge eggs or young, and send them tumbling into the sea. Instead, Kittiwakes seem just to shout abuse at their neighbours if they come too close, and the major feature of a colony must be *noise* – never are Kittiwakes silent. Each time an adult returns to the nest, there is an effusive and vociferous greeting display, with much head bowing and wing flapping, from its partner.

The Kittiwake youngsters (usually one or two in number) naturally have to be specially well-behaved, and until they fly cannot walk more than six inches from where they hatched, no matter how hungry they are, or how anxiously they watch a food-carrying par-

ent passing to and fro, choosing the right moment to attempt a landing in the tricky updraughts of the cliff face. Eventually the adult will land, and regurgitate a meal of shrimps and other planktonic delicacies, appreciatively received by the young.

A colony is well worth hours of watching. Be careful, of course, not just for *your* safety on the cliffs but that you do not disturb the birds. Watch the comings and goings through binoculars, and marvel that such graceful birds will leave the cliffs in July to spend the winter spread across the Atlantic, as far afield as the iceberg waters of the Newfoundland Banks, before they return to their colonies early next spring.

SEDGE WARBLER

Sedge Warblers are typical birds of the lush vegetation of wetland and waterside habitats. Sometimes they will encroach on the true reed beds – primarily Reed Warbler territory – but more often they occupy the drier areas, with an increasing tendency to colonise completely dry areas like young forestry plantations and crops. Thus although ancestrally birds of the swamps, they are adaptable to almost any luxuriant, slightly dank vegetation.

Ginger-brown above, with heavy black streaking; rich yellow-buff below, with a dark crown and conspicuous pale eyestripe, Sedge Warblers are easily distinguished from their cousins, the Reed Warblers, which are an all-over unstreaked olive-brown, and tend far more to be birds of extensive reed-bed areas.

Sedge Warblers have a conspicuous, Whitethroat-like, song flight, but also sing from regular 'song-post' perches, often atop a bush. The song is very varied, a tumultuous jumble of phrases, some harsh, some twangy and some melodious. It is far less repetitive than the Reed Warbler, and contains far more phrases mimicked from other marshland birds. Sedge Warblers are nocturnal migrants, the males arriving some days before the females and establishing territories. They sing a lot at night early in the season, it is thought to attract the attention of females migrating overhead.

The nest of the Sedge Warbler is well-hidden, normally situated low down in dense vegetation and far more difficult to find than the elegant basketwork structure of the Reed Warbler, neatly suspended half-way up the reed stems. Perhaps Cuckoos find the nests difficult to locate (or lay in) for although the Reed Warbler is one of the 'top three' Cuckoo foster-parents, the Sedge Warbler is only occasionally parasitised.

A successful bird, the Sedge Warbler is widely distributed. Only the Willow Warbler and the Whitethroat, of the warblers, have a more extensive range, and the Sedge Warbler is unusual for summer migrants in Ireland in that it penetrates right across to the western coast. They are impressively successful, too, as long-range migrants. Sedge Warblers winter in swampy areas of tropical Africa. Just as astonishing as the navigational ability (which enables them to reach the same wintering marsh each year) is the mechanical ability of the bird as a flying machine. 'Fuel' for the journey is carried, largely as fat deposited beneath the skin and in

the body cavity. The Sedge Warbler weighs twelve grammes or so in normal trim: before departure south in autumn, it may feed up to such an extent that its weight exceeds twenty grammes. In this state the bird appears almost spherical, with fat deposited even under the eyelids. It has been estimated that enough 'fuel' is carried for between sixty and ninety hours of non-stop flying – certainly enough to reach Africa in one hop!

SKYLARK

'Hark! Hark! The Lark at Heaven's gate sings' – wrote Shakespeare in *Cymbeline*. Surely no noise is more typical, more redolent, of the open countryside in summer than the song of the Skylark. Often this is produced at several hundred feet (not quite heaven's gate perhaps) with the songster very difficult to locate against a bright blue sky. If you can find the singer, and study him through binoculars, watch how precisely he maintains his station, hovering on quickly beating wings, tail fanned, bobbing about as if attached to the sky by a short length of elastic.

Skylarks are quite at home on any open farmland, moorland or rough grassland, and although certainly not the most numerous of British birds, are contenders for title of 'most widely distributed', as they occur throughout highlands, lowlands, and offshore islands alike. They seem to have adapted to the changes in modern farming better than any other bird, and even the despised 'prairie farming' of vast cereal acreages seems to provide a perfectly satisfactory habitat despite the insecticides and herbicides used.

The Skylark is a ground nester. The streaky browns, buffs and greys of its plumage conceal the sitting bird on its dried-grass nest admirably against the background of the soil; so well that you almost need to tread on the sitting bird to flush her. The nestlings, too, are well camouflaged, and leave the nest early, some days before they can fly. Once away from the nest the family split up and hide singly over a wide area, giving them a much better chance of escaping the attentions of predators like foxes and weasels.

Despite popular belief, Skylarks quite commonly sing from fence posts, or even from the ground, where their unexpectedly conspicuous crest, raised in song, shows up to good effect. It is often said that the ground song is different, but the difference is usually too subtle for easy detection.

Chaucer had his Knight in the *Canterbury Tales* call the Skylark 'The bisy lark – messenger of the day' – a tribute to its early rising and common presence at the very opening of the midsummer dawn chorus. Clearly, Skylarks move those of artistic temperament. Throughout history, poets have celebrated this songster, but nicest of all perhaps, the composer Ralph Vaughan Williams has captured the very essence of Skylark atmosphere – the wide open skies which are the lark's domain – in *The Lark Ascending*. For each of us, the

cheerful but rather repetitive song may lack something as sheer bird musicianship, but more than compensates by what it offers as *the* sound to relax to in summer, conveying all the atmosphere, conjuring up all the images, of our ideal countryside.

CURLEW

In summer, the Curlew is very much a bird of moorland in the west and north of Britain and Ireland. It is perhaps the most conspicuously noisy of moorland breeding birds, calling and bubbling all day – and often for much of the short midsummer night – over the heather and mosses of boggy areas. The Curlew's display must surely rank as one of *the* sights and especially sounds for the birdwatcher. The male, drab in speckled plumage of buffs, browns and blacks, jumps into the air and climbs steeply on rapidly beating wings. Once aloft, he hovers awhile, and then descends on stiff, vibrating wings, slowly like a parachute – all the time producing the most thrilling mixture of calls, gurgling, bubblings and whistlings, ending in the evocative and oft-repeated 'coo-er-leew' from which its name is derived.

The nest is always well concealed, often in a grassy tussock amongst the silver feathery plumes of bog cotton grass. For the sitting bird, the drab plumage is good camouflage, but it remains surprising that this rather gaunt, angular, gull-sized bird with disproportionately large beak can vanish so effectively when she shuffles down to incubate her black-spotted olive-brown eggs. Breeding Curlews are extremely wary. The male stands guard on a nearby hummock, sounding the alarm to call the female off the nest as soon as danger threatens. She sneaks away from the nest, long legs bent and head held close to the ground, but should the intruder continue towards the nest, the pair will start a clamour that would put a fire alarm to shame! As a further distraction, the female may even land close to a marauding fox, and stumble along dragging one wing as if injured, in an attempt to invite pursuit of herself to lure the predator away from the actual nest.

Young Curlews hatch ready-covered in camouflage down, eyes open, alert and ready to scamper about and feed themselves – vastly different from the naked, torpidly helpless and reptile-like young of the Blackbird, for example. One question must arise: how does the Curlew get its six-inch beak into a chicken-sized egg? The answer is that the Curlew hatches with a short, almost straight beak, which grows disproportionately quickly. After hatching, the two, three or four youngsters are divided between the parents on feeding expeditions. If danger threatens, the parents bark a warning and the young crouch, and remain dead still however close danger comes, relying

on their stillness and camouflage for safety.

In winter, the Curlew is an estuary bird. Our breeding population is joined by many thousands of migrants escaping from the frozen mudflats of northern Europe. The 'J' shaped beak is used to full length probing deep into the ooze for worms and, occasionally, small shellfish. Thus even those of us living distant from moorland can see Curlews in winter, and listen to a wild, but muted, variety of their calls. Even better, at a time when we look gloomily at many wild bird populations and lament their decrease, it is pleasing to report that the Curlew seems to be spreading as a breeding bird, eastward into lowland Britain. So perhaps in the not too distant future many more of us will be able to visit swampy meadows to enjoy the wildness of the Curlew's fabulous song.

PUFFIN

The handsome and charming Puffin, elegant in dinner-jacket-like black and white plumage, is one of our most popular birds, but one difficult to study in detail. Its comings and goings about the colony are notoriously fickle, and it nests in a burrow too deep and dark to permit eggs or young to be seen. From these depths, adult Puffins can be heard grumbling and groaning and producing extraordinary sepulchural moans worthy of a horror film.

Fortunately, most puffinries are large, and once the young have hatched in June, adults are always to be seen visiting their burrows with sand eels or similar small fish held crosswise in their beaks. Their carrying capacity is phenomenal. Often there will only be a dozen or so fish, but up to sixty small fry in one beakful – all held crosswise – is on record. It is still not clearly understood how the Puffin can catch more fish without dropping those it already holds. The huge, parrot-like beak, so colourful with red, blue and yellow bands in summer, grows only for display in the breeding season. The horny outer sheath is shed at the end of summer, to be replaced by a much smaller and strictly functional grey winter beak.

Most colonies are in remote, near-inaccessible places, often islands, perhaps because the Puffin is sensitive to human disturbance. This problem is increased by its liking for grassy slopes, capable of supporting sheep through the summer. In either case, it is difficult to understand the stability of colonies on remote islands like St Kilda, where for centuries the Puffin filled a vital role in human economy, many thousands being harvested for food and feathers without any long-term drop in numbers.

On land, the upright waddling stance of the Puffin, on bright orange-webbed feet, may appear comical, but it is also clumsy and renders it vulnerable to predation by Great Black-backed Gulls. Nor are they skilful fliers, being better adapted for under-water performance. They have difficulty in landing with dignity in strong crosswinds, a factor exploited by Herring Gulls, which harass the Puffin until it crash-lands, dropping its beakful of fish, which are gobbled up by the gull.

Sudden declines seem to be a feature of the Puffins' history: some perhaps due to chemical or oil pollution, or to the accidental introduction of the devastating brown rat, as on Lundy, once called 'Isle of Puffins'. It is thought that on Grassholm, off Pembrokeshire, once

a huge puffinry, over-intensive burrowing by the Puffins made the soil too friable, so that erosion by wind and water left only bedrock to the detriment of the Puffins but allowing an enormous gannetry to develop.

Some Puffins nest in holes in cliff faces, and large colonies occur in the screes at the head and foot of the cliffs. Most Puffins, though, nest in grassland burrows. They may dig these themselves, or commandeer them from rabbits or Manx Shearwaters. The grassy slopes are usually covered in pink thrift, white sea-campion, and often bluebells, all flourishing on the guano deposits and forming an attractive back-drop to the social gatherings and communal flypasts that are so much part of the Puffins' life.

TURTLE DOVE

The Bible contains several of the earliest references to bird migration, and by far the nicest is to be found in the *Song of Solomon:*

For lo, the winter is past, the rain is over and gone;
The flowers appear on the earth; the time of the
    singing of birds
        is come, and the voice of the turtle is heard in our land.

The 'turtle' referred to is *not* the marine reptile (which is more or less voiceless anyway) but the Turtle Dove, a small fast-flying pigeon. Bronze-backed and a mixture of soft fawns and pinks below, with a white-fringed tail, the Turtle Dove visits our woods and farmland in summer, having spent the winter in Africa.

The 'voice of the turtle' is a long-drawn-out, peacefully drowsy purring. In suitable areas of scrubby woodland, Turtle Doves can occur in large numbers, and on hot summer days seem able to fill the woodland airspace with their song, ventriloquial to the degree that it becomes difficult to pinpoint any individual.

Turtle Doves are primarily birds of the arable farmscape of southern and eastern England, needing open rural areas for feeding and, unlike most related pigeons, apparently quite unable to live in towns or even villages. They eat a wide variety of seeds, but fumitory is a special favourite, readily available all the time Turtle Doves are in this country. Indeed, the maps of breeding distribution of the Turtle Dove and of the occurrence of fumitory show a remarkable coincidence.

Often, small flocks of Turtle Doves may be disturbed from the gravelly surface of quiet country lanes: they love sunbathing on the warm tarmac, but also pick up sharp pieces of grit and swallow them. Birds, of course, have no teeth, so those (like the Turtle Dove) that live on tough dry seeds use this grit, in their gizzards, to help grind up their food for easier digestion.

Turtle Doves build amazingly frail platform nests, very often choosing a hawthorn bush. The nest is flat, and made of relatively few slender twigs: so few that you can usually *see* the eggs by looking up *through* the floor of the nest! How such a skimpy structure survives the beefy youngsters – usually two in number – is difficult to imagine, but it does, plus the added weight of the parent birds when they visit bringing food. Most unusually in the bird

world, pigeons produce a sort of milk – popularly called 'pigeons' milk'. This is not strictly the same as the milk of mammals, but is a highly nutritious secretion from the wall of the pigeon's crop: white in colour, hence 'milk'. On this rich diet, the young grow rapidly.

Although they are amongst the latest migrants to arrive, and breeding is usually not under way until mid- or late-May, most Turtle Dove pairs attempt to raise at least two broods, sometimes three, in their crowded stay in Britain. At the end of August, and through September, flocks of Turtle Doves will wing their way south, braving not just the natural hazards of long-distance migration, but also running the lethal gauntlet of hunters in Southern Europe, where the Turtle Dove ranks high as a tasty delicacy.

GREEN WOODPECKER

We often compare our birds unfavourably with their highly-coloured cousins from tropical areas, but few tropical birds can compete with the vivid beauty of the Green Woodpecker. Often the first view is of a pigeon-sized bird with deeply undulating flight, appearing to be made of pale gold as it swoops across the meadows. Following up for a closer view, the full beauty is revealed. It is difficult to believe that such greens and golds, set off by a scarlet cap and black, white and scarlet moustaches could ever appear on a British bird!

One of the many old colloquial names for the Green Woodpecker is 'yaffle' – a word that well describes the ringing, laughing call, as much a feature of the bird as its gorgeous plumage. The Green Woodpecker is the largest of the British woodpeckers, and paradoxically spends much of its time on the ground rather than pecking wood. What it is doing is looking for ants, and probably one of the major reasons for its scarcity now compared with as recently as twenty years ago is not so much that it tends to suffer in severe winters, but more that grassland, in general, has been much improved. Only rarely nowadays, because of myxomatosis and agricultural improvement, do we see rabbit-cropped meadows lumpy with ant hills.

Ants, their eggs and larvae, and also on occasions various insect grubs from rotten wood, are collected on the Green Woodpecker's tongue. This tongue is one of the masterpieces of evolutionary adaptation. As in all woodpeckers it is surprisingly long: it can protrude three or four inches, and when not in active use lies coiled in a tubular sheath running beneath the lower jaw and up on to the top of the skull. This long tongue can be poked down ant runs, and is covered in a copious and very sticky layer of saliva, which traps the ants and obviously so gums them up as to immobilise them. So, when they are back to feed the hungry youngsters in their nest, nobody gets bitten or squirted with formic acid.

Woodpeckers excavate their own nest holes, often in dead wood or living softwood trees, less commonly in hardwoods. The hole is chiselled, rather than hacked out, with the beak inserted into a crack and then twisted to prise off a large flake of wood. These chips are a give-away for the nest site, showing fresh and white in spring against the sombre brown background of last year's fallen leaves. A

short horizontal tunnel leads from the entrance hole to a vertical shaft several inches deep ending in the flask-shaped nest chamber. Here a few wood chips serve as nest lining for the almost spherical white eggs. Especially in their early days, the young are conspicuously ugly and reptilian: a feature enhanced by their scanty covering of down. They are very fussily noisy, and this clearly is a potentially hazardous situation if there are predators about, as the young are deep in the hole and cannot themselves see danger coming. Hence the Green Woodpecker has a considerable repertoire of stern anxiety calls to warn its young to be silent until the alarm is over.

FULMAR

Although gull-like in its white and grey plumage, a close-up view shows that the Fulmar has a more complicated beak, formed of several segments with the joints between clearly visible. On the ridge of the beak, running lengthwise, are two tubular 'nostrils', which indicates that the Fulmar belongs to the 'tube-nose' or petrel family. There is some argument whether these tubes have anything to do with smell (a sense very poorly developed in most birds) or whether perhaps they have a pressure-sensitive function that serves the Fulmar as a type of air-speed indicator.

Fulmars are master gliders, and their flight is another feature distinguishing them from gulls. Their stiff, narrow wings are held slightly downturned, and their dumpy but excellently streamlined bodies allow them to plane, skimming close to the waves. In this way they get maximum lift from the wind, and use remarkably little energy – with hardly a wing-flap except on a very still day. Even the eyes are deep-set in the feathers of the head, and the feet are usually tucked out of sight within the body feathers for better streamlining. Only near to the nesting cliffs are they extended and used for fine adjustments in manoeuvring.

The nest sites chosen are usually broad ledges, as Fulmars are clumsy on land and need adequate space for take-off and landing. Although nowhere near as noisy as Kittiwakes, they have a display chorus – often produced by several pairs at once – that sounds rather like a choir of crooning chickens! They can defend themselves well, spitting quantities of foul-smelling oily stomach contents at intruders who approach the nest too closely. This they can do accurately – even nestlings just a few days old – at a range of several feet. On the wing, too, they will attack potential predators near the nest, even those as large as Ravens and Sea Eagles, and on occasions startled and discomfited rock-climbers or innocently straying sheep. The technique is effective: once hit, the offending bird lands and starts to preen furiously, trying to keep its plumage in shape.

Perhaps it is such aggression that helps Fulmars live so long. We think that most do not breed until they are seven or eight years old, and so far, ironically, they seem to outlive the metal rings that we put on their legs to see how long they live! Certainly many must live for thirty years, and some may even live as long as we do. So even if they only lay one egg each year, it is hardly surprising that Fulmars

are on the increase. Even where there are no cliffs, like the Dungeness shingle peninsula in Kent, they take the next best man-made alternative: in the case of Dungeness, the nuclear-power-station window-sills. Obviously they are adaptable birds that should go far. This is amply demonstrated by their success story so far in Britain. In the latter part of the nineteenth century, there was only one colony on remote St Kilda in the Hebrides. The islanders depended heavily on Fulmars, 'farmed' sensibly, for food (eggs, young and adults were all eaten); for oil (to fuel lamps, cooking stoves and for medicinal purposes); and for feathers ('exported' to help pay the rent, and used to stuff army pillows). During this century, there has been a steady spread southwards, and the coasts of Britain and Ireland are now completely ringed by Fulmar colonies.

YELLOWHAMMER

Buntings as a family are hardly the avian world's best songsters, but the Yellowhammer – or Yellow Bunting – is better than most, tuneful if rather wheezy. Perhaps the wheeziness reflects the hay-fever season through which the Yellowhammer sings, as they are very much birds of the hot afternoons of high summer. Most of us were taught the human translation of the Yellowhammer jingle – 'a little bit of bread and no cheese' – at an early age, but as the Yellowhammer often leaves off the cheese, it is difficult to guess how these words were devised!

Yellowhammers are birds of open countryside – choosing conspicuous song posts like bush tops, telephone wires or fenceposts. They prefer farmland with good thick hedges, well-bushed heathland or hawthorn-rich scrubby areas in summer, but in winter are often found in open fields or on the marshes, especially around areas where sheep and cattle are fed hay.

In winter, both male and female are a yellowish fawn, with darker streaks and some rusty-red patches. They tend to flock with others of their kind, and finches and sparrows, on rough weedy ground or stubble, seeking seeds. At this time they are very inconspicuous, with only a quiet 'chip' call likely to draw your attention to them. But come the spring, what a change! For camouflage purposes, the female will retain her drab dress, but wear and tear will have worn away the buff and brown ends of the males' feathers, gradually revealing the summer plumage beneath in all its glory. Wear and tear will have also reduced the insulation properties of the plumage, ready for the warm summer weather, so this is an extremely neat multipurpose adaptation. It seems so surprising that the one piece of knowledge we all have about the Yellowhammer is its song: rarely is there any mention of its plumage except in the name *Yellow*hammer. In full plumage, perched up in the sun, a male Yellowhammer (for my money) will outdo the best of canaries. His bright yellows and golds, subtle rusts and chestnuts, will rival even the flowering gorse bushes on which he so often sits.

Cousin to the Yellowhammer, the other open-country bunting is the aptly-named Corn Bunting, which is an enigmatic bird in many ways. Its distribution is patchy, and although it seems associated with cereals, we do not fully understand why. The nest is well-concealed on the ground, and the youngsters leave before they are

fully fledged, so we have a poor knowledge of their breeding biology. Polygamy is suspected, but we are uncertain how regular this is. The plumage is hardly distinctive: both sexes remain plumply overweight and drab with streaks year-round. The song (so called) definitely fits the 'once heard never forgotten' category, tactfully described as like jangling keys, but perhaps more akin to a tin tray sliding about on broken glass.

RED GROUSE

The Red Grouse has often been considered as the only bird exclusively restricted to Britain and Ireland, but expert opinion now supports the view that it is only a distinct race of the Willow Grouse or Willow Ptarmigan, which is widespread in northern Europe and North America.

Dark reddish-brown, seeming almost black at a distance, the cock Red Grouse standing on a hummock or boulder is a characteristic bird of open treeless moorland. Grouse tend to remain in concealment, crouched in the heather, until you almost step on them. Then they 'explode' in a heart-stopping flurry, whirring away on down-curved wings, cackling angrily, showing their white-feathered legs. The display song can be written, 'go back, go back, back, back, grrrr . . .'

Grouse are heavily dependent on heather shoots for food, with other moorland plants like crowberry and bilberry providing occasional alternatives. The number on any particular moor is partly determined by the nature of the soil – in limestone areas, numbers tend to be high, while they are lowest on thick peats overlying granite. They are game birds, and like others of their kind are shot for sport and because they are remarkably tasty to eat. In sporting circles, 12 August – the glorious twelfth – is one of the red-letter days. For this reason, besides variations in their natural habitat, Grouse numbers are very much influenced by man.

The shoots, in which lines of beaters drive the birds over guns concealed in butts, used to be the province of the landed gentry. Now the ownership of a grouse moor has become a most effective land use – in financial terms – as the return from renting out the shooting is far higher than from any agricultural use. Whatever one may think of shooting, the sport does coincidentally ensure the continued maintenance and survival of this type of moorland – a valuable service to the environment.

Grouse 'bags' have decreased markedly in recent years. It was thought initially that disease and predation were responsible, which generated an intensification of the persecution by gamekeepers of birds of prey of all sizes, from Merlins to Golden Eagles. We now know that predation affects only the non-breeding surplus and does not affect the shooting season: what has been clearly shown is that the major reason for the decline is the deterio-

ration of management and thus heather quality. Heather moorland requires intensive keepering: drainage, fertiliser application and restrictions on grazing all have to be supervised. Above all, areas have to be burnt, in rotation, to ensure a continuous succession of young heather shoots for food.

The balance of new and old heather must be carefully watched, as the deeper growth provides shelter and nest sites. Here the well-camouflaged female will incubate her dark reddish eggs for almost four weeks. Once the young hatch, they quickly leave the nest, and as with many game birds, are able to fly at about two weeks, long before they are full-grown.

GOLDFINCH

The Goldfinch is very much the harlequin of the bird world, with black cap, red and white face, pale buff belly and black wings with the broadest bar of pure gold feathers. Perhaps they are seen at their best on the thistle-heads of late summer, with their colours set off against green leaves and purple flowers.

As they move from seed-head to seed-head, the continuous sparkling of colours gives a clue to the origins of the collective noun for a group of Goldfinches – a 'charm'. The word could equally well apply to the song, typically with a few warming-up notes to clear the throat preceding an extended tinkling trill. Obviously a bird with such a variety of attractions to human eyes and ears runs the tragic risk of its beauty being its undoing. For the Goldfinch this is indeed the case: in Britain until quite recently and on the Continent (Belgium particularly) even today, tens of thousands of Goldfinches are trapped each year and caged. Despite the efforts of the Royal Society for the Protection of Birds, in Britain even now an illegal and unsavoury black-market bird-catching trade persists. Such activities are difficult to track down, and it is to be hoped that new legislation on cage-bird breeding and exhibtion will help to eradicate it entirely.

In autumn and winter, Goldfinches use the very slender tips to their beaks – still conical or wedge-shaped like other seed-eaters, but with the tips elongated almost like a pair of tweezers – to extract seeds from plants protected so well by their prickles that other finches cannot tackle them. The sight of a group of Goldfinches, on a winter's day, disturbing tufts of thistledown to blow away on the wind or bejewelling the teazel heads is a sure reminder that summer will come again.

Goldfinches are birds of rough ground and scrub and penetrate our gardens relatively infrequently. Their cousins, the Greenfinches, although ancestrally also birds of scrub and forest edge, have taken very readily to our gardens. Their drowsy purring song is as much a part of a hot summer weekend in suburbia as is the chink of teacup on saucer or the chatter of lawnmowers! Often the male Greenfinch will sing on the wing, in a circling display flight with wings beating so exaggeratedly slowly that it is called the 'butterfly' display. This is the best time to see the golden dusting to his green plumage and the bold yellow patches in his tail as he fans it to bank

and turn.

Although Greenfinches will feed with other finches on weed seeds in stubble and fallow fields, their presence in gardens has opened up another food source. When peanuts for winter bird-feeding became readily available, Greenfinches were not slow on the uptake, much quicker than Sparrows. So quickly has the habit spread that Greenfinches are among the most regular feeders in our gardens, as agile even as tits on the peanut-holders.

KINGFISHER

Often all that we see of a Kingfisher is an electric-blue arrow, shooting past on whirring wings low over the water, jinking at the last minute to avoid overhanging branches. Should you be lucky enough to see one perched on a post or a branch overlooking the water, then the full truth of Gerard Manley Hopkins' statement 'As Kingfishers catch fire' becomes apparent when the brilliantly iridescent-blue back is suddenly turned away as the bird changes position, revealing the full glory of its bright chestnut breast and belly.

A close-up view, too, allows inspection of this striking bird, which is smaller than a thrush. The purposeful head and beak is disproportionately large compared to the body, and the tiny blood-red feet are so small they are often difficult to see. From such a perch, overlooking a favoured fishing place, Kingfishers wait and watch, the occasional bob of the head revealing more plainly the white half-collar. This is probably a gesture designed to alert other Kingfishers nearby, and warn them off its stretch of fishing water.

Once a small fish is spotted, the Kingfisher will plunge, often submerging totally before emerging, almost vertically, shaking off water droplets and heading speedily for a good perch. There, with a few deft thwacks on the branch, the fish is stunned or killed and swallowed whole, headfirst. The dive may often be at a shallow angle to a fish twenty or thirty feet away, a tribute to the Kingfisher's keen eyesight.

Kingfishers are birds of placid, reed-fringed lakes or clear streams with plenty of overhanging vegetation, and with stretches of low earthen cliffs suitable for nesting. According to the ancients, the Kingfisher – called 'Halcyon' – made a nest of fishbones and launched it on the sea. While she was brooding, the gods ordered that the oceans be calmed. Pliny, normally an acute observer of natural history, wrote (at about the time of the birth of Christ) 'they breed in winter, at a season called *the halcyon days,* wherein the sea is calm and fit for navigation'. Ideas about these fabled halcyon days persisted until Michael Drayton, who at the end of the sixteenth century wrote:

> 'Then came the halcyon whom the sea obeys
> When she her nest upon the water lays'

In actuality, the nest is anything but halcyon. Kingfishers breed during the summer, excavating a tunnel up to a yard long in a suitable bank. In a chamber at the end of this lies the nest – made of fishbones yes, but dark, slimy, noisy and above all smelling power-fully of aged fish and the droppings of the young. So revolting is it that the parents often dunk themselves in the water immediately after leaving the tunnel to remove the scales and slime.

LAPWING

Lapwing, Green Plover, Peewit: just three of the colloquial names for this popular bird – which shows how confusing local names can be. Each name, though, has its point: Peewit clearly comes from the plaintive, rasping cry so familiar over meadows and marshes. Green Plover, too, is appropriate. Take a close-up look at that apparently black-and-white bird on a sunny day: the back is deepest bottle-green, shot with iridescent purples, and really beautiful.

Often you will see Lapwings in the air, when their very floppy, clumsy-looking flight gives a clear indication of how the name 'Lapwing' was derived. In winter, Lapwings react very quickly to changes in the weather, and any really cold spell is first heralded for the birdwatcher by flocks of Lapwings, flickering black and white across a stormy sky, heading westward towards warmer weather.

Closer to, the rounded wings produce a marked whooshing noise specially their own. In the breeding season, this wing noise comes into its own as a terror weapon to repel invaders, in just the same way as screaming dive-bombers were used in wartime. Any marauding fox or crow – or even human – is instantly attacked as it enters the breeding territory. The swooping, screeching Lapwings, with these thumping wingbeats, are usually enough to put off – or at least distract – any predator and ensure the safety of the nest. The sight of a harmless pair of Partridges, straying accidentally into a Lapwing territory and then attempting to withdraw, with dignity, under such an onslaught, is one to be savoured.

The nest itself is a mere scrape in the ground, neatly lined with grass and, almost inevitably, containing four sharply-pointed eggs, arranged points inward in a neat square. The shape of the eggs is distinctive, and has a logical explanation. Young Lapwing hatch down-covered, and as soon as they are dry, will scamper around fending for themselves under the watchful eyes of their parents. This demands precociously well-developed legs, and these are housed, compactly folded, in the pointed part of the egg.

Although the sitting bird may seem conspicuous in the middle of a field, she will slip off the nest if danger appears, and once she is away, the eggs are so well camouflaged as to be difficult to find. Each parent usually copes with two chicks. They, too, are well camouflaged and squat down when their parents shout a warning at them, not moving until your foot is within inches.

Lapwings are classed among the wading birds, but unlike most, their prime habitat is *not* the shore. Their short beaks are ideal for catching insects and the like, and most breed on moorland, rough grassland or farmland. In winter, most will be found on damp grassland or plough, and it is amazing to see how a flock of conspicuously black-and-white birds can apparently vanish into the ground when they land. It is well worth seeking a closer look (using a car as a hide is a good idea) to appreciate the beauty of the long uptilted crest and the sheen of the feathers.

Towards the end of the winter, these flocks will disperse, spring will return and the Lapwings will take up their territories, and the air will again be full of tumbling, calling birds performing their aerobatic displays.

SWALLOW

One Swallow does not make a summer, the saying goes. True enough, but how much pleasanter summers are for the presence of Swallows around our homes! Perhaps the saying more reflects the fact that although the occasional Swallow may arrive late in March, the bulk of its fellows sensibly wait until April is established, and warmer weather has provided adequate insect supplies to keep them fed.

Swallows have an amazing migration – travelling north each spring from wintering areas in the extreme south of Africa. A prodigious journey, carried out at high speed, but at least Swallows, as aerial feeders, can refuel in mid-air! Today we put numbered light-alloy rings on birds' legs to help trace their migratory routes and establish journey times, but marked Swallows were used as far back as the Punic wars in 300 BC in the role of carrier pigeons. Adult Swallows were taken from their nestlings and smuggled out of besieged garrisons: they were later released, to 'home' to their nests, with a message attached to their legs giving details of the relief force's progress. Shortly after, the results of chariot races in Rome were conveyed to Volterra – one hundred and twenty miles away – quickly and effectively by tying threads of the winners' colours to the Swallow's leg.

The nest is made of small mud pellets, picked up in the beak from the edge of a puddle, and stuck on a beam or under the eaves of an infrequently used building. This mud-brick structure, shaped like a half-cup, is reinforced with strands of dried grass and neatly lined with hair and feathers. In a fine summer, the first young may be heard squeaking faintly early in May.

Despite a tight-packed breeding season, with at least two and often three broods of young being reared, the male has time to sing from the wires right through the summer. Sometimes the nest can get a little crowded, especially in cool, wet summers. Shortage of food and cold nights keep the first brood close to the nest site, although they can fly freely and care for themselves. At night, they may all cram onto the nest with the second brood, often with the female sitting uncomfortably on top – perhaps ten or a dozen birds – which says a lot for their building technique.

As summer draws to a close, gatherings of Swallows on wires or rooftops – soaking up the sun – become more and more frequent.

Often enough, they are parties that will migrate south together, facing the hazards of crossing mountains, seas and deserts. But one of the nicest things that bird-ringing has shown is that the chances of *your* adult Swallows returning to *your* shed or garage are high – so the bird you see next spring is likely to be an old friend.

STARLING

The Starling must be one of the few birds as familiar to office workers in cities as it is to countrymen. Many city statues and window-ledges support roosting Starlings in considerable warmth (3° warmer than in the country), and the half-hour before a winter sunset will see wheeling mobs circling over the city squares. Once perched, they do not 'switch out the light and go to sleep' but continue to chatter − a noise that has given rise to the collective noun − very picturesque − for such gatherings: a *murmuration* of Starlings.

Of course country roosts do occur, often larger than city ones and very destructive of the patch of woodland chosen. The noise, often of several hundreds of thousands of birds, is as spectacular as the mass aerobatics as they come in to roost, and the smell within the roost is on the same grand scale! Such is the size of roosts that they are visible on airfield radar screens, and the periodic departures of groups of birds in the morning has its own name. Bird echoes on radar are called 'angels', and Starlings, leaving in all directions from a roost, do so in pulses, giving an image of concentric rings (like those produced by dropping a pebble in a pool), and hence are called 'ring angels'. A sudden cessation of chatter, a brief silence, and then a roar of wings heralds each departing group.

When they get to their food, be it in the fields or on our garden bird tables, Starlings continue to be noisily gregarious. There is much apparent aggression, with birds shaping up to each other with feathers bristling and little hops of anger into the air. Although they may seem to be greedy bullies, their technique has to be admired and they are *very* successful birds.

Although in winter they may compete with chickens, and even cattle, for the food put out by farmers, we should not forget that an awful lot of leatherjackets and other soil pests vanish down Starlings' greedy throats. The good that they do is difficult to value, but the damage that a flock of noisy 'teenagers' can do to a cherry crop in summer is all too easily seen.

Starlings will nest in any sort of cavity: a nestbox, second-hand woodpecker holes, and commonly under the eaves of houses, where a feeding parent returning to raucous hungry young may waken us soon after first light. You can recognise the sexes in summer: *his* yellow beak is blue at the base, *hers* is tinged with pink. Sitting on

the roof, or on a phone wire, you can admire his iridescent beauty as he sings, bolt upright, throat feathers bristling, flapping his wings in slow-motion display.

They really are superb mimics, and often by listening to the song you can tell where else the bird has been. Many of our winter-visitor Starlings breed in Poland, and careful listening may reveal snatches of mimicry of the Golden Oriole, a bird rare in Britain but common in eastern Europe, woven into the Starling's song. Perhaps it was their cheerful song that prompted our forefathers to take Starlings all over the world as they colonised it. Almost everywhere, Asia, America, Australasia, the Starlings were so successful that they soon became troublesome. Even so, you cannot help a sneaking liking for Starlings – quarrelsome, bumptious, swashbuckling, and strikingly beautiful close to.

ARCTIC TERN

The terns, aptly given the popular name 'sea swallows', are perhaps the most graceful and elegant of our seabirds. Silver-grey and white, with darker wing-tips and black cap, and long swallow-like tail streamers, they are smaller and much slimmer than any of the gulls. All are migrants, travelling to fish in the oceans of the southern hemisphere during the winter, returning to our coasts to breed in summer.

The Arctic Tern probably sees more hours of daylight each year than any other creature. Arctic Terns breed in northern Britain, and further north up into the Arctic Circle, where the summer is virtually without darkness. Having raised their young on the short-lived summer abundance of insects and fish, they migrate southwards, crossing the equator to spend our winter in the Antarctic Ocean. Here again they have the benefit of almost perpetual daylight, and enjoy an immensely rich food supply of small fish and plankton.

During the breeding season, terns fish close inshore, flickering along lazily in the air a few feet above the waves before suddenly turning and plunging headlong into the sea. Often these dives result in an audible 'plop' and a considerable splash, but the bird penetrates only a few inches rather than submerging deeply. The prey is usually small fish or shrimps, and these are taken (one at a time, not in a beakful like the Puffin) back to the colony. Early in the season, the male will often bring a fish back to his mate, standing at the shallow scrape which serves for a nest.

All the terns are colonial breeders, and the colonies may be thousands strong. Very often they are located on remote beaches or sand dunes, or on small islands that offer the greatest security from human disturbance and from predators like foxes or hedgehogs, which have a taste for eggs. Eggs and young alike are perfectly camouflaged against the background of sand flecked with fragments of seaweed and shell. Although the colonies seem close-packed, terns are vociferously abusive neighbours and squabbles are common, so closer inspection will reveal that nests are always at least two beak-thrusts apart!

The oldest Arctic Tern that we know of was a ringed bird that lived for twenty-six years. Travelling almost from pole to pole twice each year, its lifetime mileage is unthinkably high: certainly several million miles. Ringed Common Terns (a close relative) from

Great Britain have been found in Australia, but despite this propensity for long-distance travel terns can often be seen feeding close inshore near to many of our coastal holiday resorts.

MALLARD

So common are Mallard, not just on village ponds but on any stretch of water, even a park lake deep in the centre of a city, that it is tempting to assume that they are semi-domesticated. They seem to be tame, and largely dependent on small children (and many grown-ups!) for liberal supplies of bread to keep body and soul together. Whilst it may be true that we allow ourselves to be exploited by these town-dwelling Mallard, most are genuinely wild birds spending parts of the year in the remote open spaces of our rivers and estuaries, or migrating across northern Europe to distant breeding grounds.

As they are often so tame, Mallard allow us to take a close-up interest in their lives without our disturbing them. Both sexes are vocal during the courtship period, the drake using a monosyllabic 'quark', the duck a rapid and strident series of 'quack-ack-acks'. Display starts before Christmas, the drake showing off his buffs and browns, curly black tail and bottle-green head to best advantage. He calls the female with an improbable-sounding whistle, and there may be excited chases on the water and in the air. When the duck is ready to mate, she signals this to the male by coyly bobbing her head to one side as she swims. Sometimes the weight of the drake as he mounts her submerges the duck entirely as mating takes place. After, the drake swims in a rapid circle round his female before both bathe vigorously.

Once mating has taken place, the drake takes no further interest in the proceedings, and the duck becomes a one-parent family. Her plumage, apparently so drab in comparison to her mate, is ideally suited to camouflage her for the long month she must spend incubating. Even before they hatch, the duck can hear the ducklings inside the eggshell. Broods are often large – a dozen ducklings or more is commonplace. Unlike Blackbirds, for example, which hatch naked, blind and helpless, ducklings emerge with their eyes open, legs well developed, and with a warm and waterproof covering of down. After a few hours, they can feed themselves on small insects on the water surface, under the watchful eye of their mother, who will dabble through the waterweed, up-ending occasionally in typical Mallard fashion.

Many hazards face the young ducklings: Swans, Coots and Moorhens – even other ducks – will take a peck at them if they come

too close. Pike and large trout fancy them for a quick snack, leaving only a tell-tale ripple to show where they were. Weirs and waterfalls wait to trap the unwary duckling that strays too far from its mother. The high-pitched worried piping of a lost chick is very much a feature of summer on the pond, before the mother, with urgent quacks, summons her brood – pattering across the water to safety at her side.

MAGPIE

'One for sorrow, two for joy' goes a version of a rhyme centred on the Magpie. Our folklore is rich in references to the Magpie, but unlike most birds it is involved with both good and evil omens. The origin of this superstition, like many others, is obscure. It may be that the boldly black-and-white plumage and the very long tail, black shot with iridescent greens and purples, and harsh chattering calls combine to make the Magpie one of the most conspicuous – and thus one of the best-known – of our birds and therefore a likely focus for legend. The nest is almost as conspicuous as the birds, a football-sized, domed construction of thorny twigs built high in a tree.

Magpies range over pretty well all types of habitat so long as there are some sheltering trees or bushes within reach, but seem to show a preference for scrub and rough farmland with grassy fields and thick hedges and thickets. They tend to avoid prairie farmland and treeless marshes, and occur mostly round the edges of large tracts of dense woodland, rarely penetrating where there are no clearings. They do, however, successfully penetrate suburban areas, town parks and large gardens, and even some city centres.

Their present-day distribution has largely been shaped by man. During Victorian times, Magpies were commonly shot and trapped, especially in game-rearing areas, where their habit of eating young birds or eggs (of any species that they came across) led almost to their elimination. Even today, the Magpie is regularly shot and is often the commonest victim on the gamekeeper's gibbet. The diet is composed primarily of various invertebrate animals – mostly insect larvae and worms, augmented by carrion, cereal seeds, fruit and berries and the occasional unwary small mammal. In short, an excellent example of an omnivore, eating whatever can be easily obtained. On the ground, they will walk along sedately searching for food, breaking into a series of bouncing hops when speed is necessary. They extend their search for insects by looking for fly maggots in the fleece of sheep, and often seem to use 'sheep-back' as a mobile vantage point to look for prey in the grass below.

The Magpie has shown itself well able to adapt to modern life, scavenging for food on town outskirts and rubbish tips, and secretively visiting garden bird tables, usually at first light. The legend of the 'Thieving Magpie' refers to the habit of Magpies (and other members of the crow family) of collecting bright objects: this habit

is difficult to explain – maybe they are for nest ornamentation, or maybe the Magpie is just being inquisitive. Such opportunism (and theft) can pay off: in Manchester, Magpies have learnt to relate milkmen to the egg-cartons they often deliver, and there are now many angry households where these have been opened, and the contents consumed, early in the morning and right on the doorstep!

DIPPER

The Dipper is very much a bird of sparkling streams flowing over shallow, pebbly rapids, and with a plentiful supply of large boulders for perches. Thus it is common in the uplands of Britain, especially in the west and north. Occasional sightings on the slower, murkier streams of the south-east, or on the coast, are usually in winter and probably these birds are stray migrants from the Continent. Dippers are thrush-sized but wren-shaped, and characteristically perch on boulders in mid-stream, tail cocked, bobbing up and down. They are a dark, rich brown, but with a chestnut-fringed large white bib, made the more conspicuous by bobbing. If alarmed, the Dipper will fly off, zooming swift and low on disproportionately small wings to less disturbed fishing.

When perched on its slippery boulder, the feet seem over-large and powerful – but with good reason, as the Dipper has a fascinating feeding technique. As you watch, it slips off its boulder and submerges in the torrent with hardly a ripple. Once beneath the surface, it feeds on small fish and various freshwater invertebrates like caddis fly larvae, shrimps, worms, shellfish and water scorpions. To catch these, often it will walk along the bottom, hanging on with those powerful feet to resist the effects of its natural buoyancy and the current. In deeper water it may leave go of the bottom and swim, using its wings for propulsion, and often appearing silvery as it is encased in a thin sheath of air-bubble.

Occasionally you will see a Dipper wink a white eyelid at you: closer inspection will show that this white eyelid travels fore-and-aft, not up-and-down. It is, in fact, the 'third eyelid' or nictitating membrane, which serves to clean the eye surface and protect it underwater.

Dippers nest early, sometimes even in February but often in March. They start singing, a *sotto-voce* melodious warbling, often difficult to locate, in late autumn and continue until midsummer. Unusually, but pleasantly, both sexes take part. The nest is usually a bulky ball of moss and grass, a super-sized Wren's nest, nowadays most often located in a cavity in the brickwork or on one of the girders beneath a bridge. Natural sites are also frequently used, such as a crevice in the bank or among the roots of an overturned tree, and in these cases the nest may be remarkably skilfully concealed. In one such case, the river rose in spate, but the nest was

protected in an airpocket by the overcurling lip of the bank. Despite apparently insurmountable problems, the adults were able to locate the nest and feed the young by diving under the lip and surfacing into the air pocket. The young eventually fledged successfully.

Dippers usually maintain their territory of half a mile or so of river, throughout the year. Normally their streams are in areas safe from industrial pollution, and the only real threat they face is a severe freeze. Then, birds on exposed Highland streams may perish, or move to a lower altitude. On these lower waters there are many records of Dippers feeding successfully beneath a surface layer of ice.

HERON

Watching a single Heron pace sedately – even stealthily – round the edge of a lake in winter, always noiseless and often motionless as it looks for an unwary fish, it is difficult to believe what a noisily boisterous life Herons lead during the breeding season. Most of our Herons nest colonially in heronries, which may contain just a few, or as many as a couple of hundred nests. Most often these are in tall trees, but occasionally in reedbeds, always within a short flight of freshwater marshes with dykes and drains full of the fish, eels and frogs that are their main diet. This menu may be augmented by water voles, snakes and even duckling, Moorhen or Dabchick that carelessly stray within reach of the swiftly stabbing beak.

In a mild winter, the first males will be about the colony in February, advertising their presence with harsh calls. Most heronries have been in existence for many years, some for centuries, like that at Chilham in Kent, which is noted in Kirkby's *Inquest*, a manuscript published in about 1290 in the reign of Edward I. It is fascinating to see that today, almost seven hundred years later, its size and location are very much the same.

Usually the oldest nests are in plum sites, huge in size from the annual addition of branches, lodged in a secure fork sheltered from chill winds and bathed in sunshine. These will be occupied by the oldest and most experienced pairs, while newcomers to the heronry will build see-through affairs with little more than a few crossed branches and twigs to support the eggs.

During their display, the Heron pair really are astonishingly noisy, honking, gurgling and shrieking. Once the eggs are laid, they are incubated in turn by the parents, and an equally noisy greeting display takes place each time there is a change-over of duty. At such times, Herons spread their huge wings wide, raise their crests and fluff out their throat feathers. Their beaks – a bright yellow for the duration of the breeding season – flush an attractive orange at the same time, and a pair rattle their beaks together in mock sword play. For such large, long-legged and apparently awkward birds, Herons get about very nimbly among the slender twigs of the canopy.

You can always tell when there are young in a heronry by their monotonous 'tack tack tack' hunger call. They always seem to be hungry – and as there may be as many as four or five nestlings, their

parents have their work cut out keeping them fed, especially in large colonies, where they may have to fly a few miles to find a free stretch of water for fishing. The parents regurgitate a crop full of eels, fish and frogs – often not quite dead – in to the bottom of the nest, adding a further guttural dimension to the extraordinary cacophony that is everyday life in a heronry.

GOLDCREST

Goldcrests are perhaps *the* typical birds of coniferous woodland and forest in Britain, no matter how densely planted and dark the trees or how 'commercial' the forest management. In parts of eastern England where conifers are scarce, they are often found in churchyard yews or in the well-grown conifers of large gardens. Populations in deciduous woodland are usually much smaller, but after a succession of mild winters, the Goldcrest population tends to 'explode', and even lowland oakwoods will support a flourishing population.

The Goldcrest is our smallest bird, weighing only about five grammes (or six to the ounce!). They are neatly rotund and fluffy, with incredibly slender legs. Greenish above, paler below, they resemble Willow Warblers and Chiffchaffs, save for a pale wing-bar and the black-edged yellow stripe on the crown that gives the bird its name. Displaying males can open out this crown stripe, and the pale yellow band then reveals its glorious flame-coloured inner recesses.

Despite their small size some are long-range migrants, and ringing recoveries tell us that our own, sedentary, population is augmented each autumn by birds from as far afield as eastern Europe. Their reasons for escaping the routinely hard winter on the Continent are plain to see when we have a severe winter in Britain. The Goldcrest is one of the first birds to suffer, and losses may be severe, certainly well in excess of 50% mortality. Fortunately, recovery is very swift, and normality is restored after only a year or two.

The song is extremely high pitched: one of the first signs of age in a birdwatcher comes when visiting conifer woodland in spring and *not* hearing a Goldcrest, as the frequency range of the human ear contracts with age. The song is a pulsating series of squeaks, terminating in a (very treble) Chaffinch-like flourish.

The birds themselves are often difficult to spot, flitting about high up in evergreens. They are confiding, though, and a while spent quietly waiting will almost always produce a worthwhile view. The nest, too, is well concealed, partly because of its unusual construction. It is a tiny basket of moss, held together with cobweb strands, and suspended, hammock-like, beneath the angle between two branches. Although the eggs (usually about eight, sometimes more)

are extraordinarily tiny and lightweight, it remains amazing that the cobweb 'handles' easily support the weight of the full-grown brood of young.

The greatly increased area of conifers in Britain resulting from the afforestation programmes of recent decades has, without doubt, benefited the Goldcrest by providing an expanse of optimal habitat for breeding and offering good winter shelter and plentiful insect food. Recent colonisations by the Goldcrest of the Scilly Isles and the Shetlands are both as a result of new conifer plantations, and many of us with maturing 'leylandii' hedges are now finding the tiny Goldcrest a familiar garden bird.

COLLARED DOVE

Back in the mid-fifties, all birdwatchers wondered just what species might be affected by the arrival of an unexpected newcomer to Britain, the Collared Dove. Would the Turtle Dove, similar in size but more richly coloured than the pale beige Collared Dove, be displaced? However, when Collared Doves arrived, they found an 'ecological niche' not otherwise occupied: a situation ripe for exploitation. In the absence of competition, the next few years saw them demonstrate just how rapidly a bird population could expand. So far as we can judge, Turtle Dove populations have been quite uninfluenced by the new arrival. The only bird that might have suffered slightly is the Woodpigeon, in that its own expansion into our towns may have been halted by the Collared Dove's arrival.

Very much a town bird, with us year-round, the Collared Dove seems always to be associated with mankind, especially in areas where grain is readily available. Most grain stores now have a resident population, as do most poultry farms. Interestingly, many of the early records in Britain were of birds closely associated with domestic chickens and the easy feeding available. Little was it guessed that a decade later, Collared Dove numbers would have exploded to the degree that, because of their pillaging of grain, they would be officially classified as *pests* in some areas.

Certainly they seem able to breed in almost any month – even sitting shrouded in snow – and almost anywhere: there is one record of a nest made of wire clippings! Most of us must by now be familiar with the wheezing flight call – an 'aaaah' uttered just before alighting on a television aerial – and the song, a 'cooh *cooh* coo', sounding like a Woodpigeon with a mouthful of spaghetti.

Whatever you may think of its habits, or the quality of its song, the rise of the Collared Dove is one of the most fascinating bird stories. They are widespread, and often very numerous, in Asia and Africa. In the thirties, for reasons we do not fully understand, but perhaps associated with a genetic mutation, an explosive expansion began. Collared Doves spread rapidly westward, establishing breeding populations as they went. By the mid-fifties they had reached Britain, and a pair bred in Norfolk in 1955, shrouded in intense secrecy. They bred again in 1956, joined by a few pairs elsewhere in south-eastern England. Secrecy was maintained, and local birdwatchers mounted guard on nest sites, straining eyes and ears for the signs

that the nest (often deep in the gloom of an old cypress) had been successful. Looking back, with the bird as common as it now is, this episode takes on a slightly hilarious aspect. In many parts of their range, Collared Doves are called Laughing Doves – perhaps they secretly enjoyed it all.

Since the touchdown in Britain, Collared Doves spread rapidly. They were breeding in western Ireland and in the Hebrides by the late sixties. By 1970, or thereabouts, Iceland and the Faeroes had been reached and conquered, and a couple of years later, they were recorded in Greenland! Where will it end? Such is the prodigious dynamism of the species that it may not be too rash to predict that, soon, Americans too might wake up to the Collared Dove's unmelodious greeting.

BLACKCAP

We generally regard warblers as sensible birds that migrate to Africa each year to escape the rigours of our winter. While this remains true for the majority, the Blackcap can be one of the exceptions. Blackcaps have never wintered as far south as most other warblers: many can be heard in song in the scrub oaks of most Mediterranean island hillsides for much of the winter, and relatively few will penetrate south of the Sahara Desert. Some of these Mediterranean birds will remain to breed on the same island in the summer, and it seems that this sedentary, rather than migratory, habit is spreading. Increasing numbers of Blackcaps are tending to spend the winter in Britain, and especially perhaps in Ireland where the climate in winter is even more bland. It may be that a succession of mild winters, with no prolonged cold spells, has fostered this habit.

In winter, Blackcaps tend to move into our gardens, feeding on the berries of ornamental shrubs like Cotoneaster, and frequently visiting bird tables for scraps: they have a particular love of suet. Both male and female are Great Tit-sized, and largely olive grey in colour. He has the coal-black cap that gives the species its name, and is often mistaken for the smaller, plumper and browner Marsh and Willow Tits. The female has a distinctive rich chestnut cap. They are aggressive at the bird table, often driving off other birds even as large and domineering as Starlings, warning them to keep away with a series of scolding 'chack' calls.

In summer, Blackcaps prefer the tall trees of mature deciduous woodlands, chosing song posts high up in the canopy. The closely-related Garden Warbler, of similar size and colour but lacking any form of cap, and with a very similar song, is far more a bird of dense undergrowth or scrub. The Blackcap song in spring is largely territorial in function, designed partly to attract a mate and partly to advertise the boundaries of that particular bird's territory.

Later in the summer, and perhaps also when recently-fledged birds are trying out their voices, Blackcaps can be seen (after a stealthy approach) sitting deep in cover singing, it appears, quietly to themselves. Such song seems to be produced almost under the breath, and the bird producing it seems totally relaxed: you could easily imagine it reclining in a deckchair in the sun! Quite what the function of this 'sub-song' is has not accurately been determined. It

may genuinely reflect a time of relaxation when the pressures of the breeding season are receding. We know that in many species, mimicry of other kinds of birds plays a part in the structure of the song: the Blackcap certainly does this, and it may well be that 'sub-song' is a time of singing practice and experimentation for younger birds, eager to impress in full song next summer.

KESTREL

Often locally, and appropriately, called 'windhover', the Kestrel is our most familiar bird of prey. One of the seemingly few environmental benefits of our motorway network is that Kestrels have quickly adapted to hunting over the new territory opened up in broad grassy verges and embankments – and it is here that most are seen. Sadly, motorways do *not* lend themselves to close observation of the Kestrel's hunting technique! This is well worth watching, through binoculars, in a more suitable location. Notice how the kestrel hangs head into wind, wings beating rapidly on calm days, but with less movement in strong winds. Despite the violent gyrations of body and tail to cope with changing winds, the head always remains rock-steady, eyes focusing downwards in search of prey. Kestrels will hover at any height, and it it no surprise to see one at a hundred feet or more: all you can do is to marvel at the acuity of eyesight that allows prey as small as a beetle to be spotted at that range.

Once the prey is in its sights, the Kestrel plummets down, braking sharply, wings outstretched at the last minute, before seizing the prey in its powerful talons. Usually one of the sharp claws pierces a vital organ as the life is crushed out of the victim, but occasionally larger prey may be killed or decapitated in typical falcon fashion with a bite at the base of the skull. In many areas, voles and mice are the main prey, but these are often augmented by less glamorous snacks like beetles and worms. Urban Kestrels prey largely on small birds.

The Kestrel, about the size of a pigeon, is the most widespread and numerous raptor in Britain, although in some western areas it may be locally outnumbered by the Sparrowhawk – rounder-winged and preferring woodland habitats. Kestrels breed in a wide range of habitats: farmland, parks, moorland, sea cliffs, woodland margins and even deep in the heart of a city. Their choice of nest site is similarly broad, including holes in trees, holes and ledges on cliffs and quarries (and even buildings, including the window-sills of high-rise flats) and in disused crows' nests.

Worrying decreases in Kestrel numbers were detected in the 1950s and 1960s, and post-mortem examinations indicated that often poisoning by some persistent organo-chlorine pesticides was the cause of death. As in the case of the Peregrine Falcon and

Sparrowhawk, the unforeseen persistence of these agricultural chemicals and the long-term build-up of toxic properties in food chains was held to be responsible for the decline. Such materials are now rarely, if ever, used, but the recovery of Kestrel numbers (especially in eastern England) is not as rapid as had been hoped. This may in part reflect a loss of nesting sites as over this wide region of intensive arable farming, hedges, trees and old buildings are removed in the cause of increased agricultural efficiency. If this is the case, we should do well to copy the Dutch. In the newly-created and treeless farmscape of the Polders, large numbers of nestboxes for Kestrels were erected on poles. An incipient plague of voles was halted, clearly demonstrating the useful role that the Kestrel plays in keeping such pests under control.

BLUE TIT

Bird-watching from the house is rarely as dull as might be supposed, especially if there is a feeding table to act as a centre of interest. At this time of year, a bird table would offer an excellent chance of seeing a Blue Tit, scolding noisily and trying to keep all the food to itself. Few of us – unless we live on the remoter islands to the north and west of Scotland – are likely to escape seeing Blue Tits. They are small birds, bright blue and green above, with a startling electric-blue cap over a white face, and with a yellow tummy. Strange to think how few birds in Britain have bright blue in their plumage.

Blue Tits are fabulously agile feeders, perhaps the most nimble of all. They have no problems hanging upside-down on swinging fat, peanuts or coconut in the garden, even sometimes by one foot! Perhaps this should not be surprising, as their natural habit is to feed at the extreme ends of branches. Most of the time, by far, they are seeking out insects when probing round the plants in the garden. In the summer, they do a tremendous job for the gardener on aphids and caterpillars, and in winter, when you may suspect them of attacking your prize buds, they are just seeking insects or their eggs or larvae, tucked into crevices in the bark.

They are more of a problem to man – and indeed are notorious – in rural and, often, urban areas too, for their attacks on milk bottles. Back in the thirties, some bright Blue Tit learnt to penetrate the cardboard cap of milk bottles to reach the cream. The habit spread remarkably quickly, and the change to aluminium foil caps posed absolutely no problem. In many areas, protection with an up-turned beaker is the only solution.

Blue Tits will use any hollow or crevice of appropriate size and reasonably sheltered, natural or man-made, as a nest site, even including drain pipes. One man-made site often used nowadays is a nestbox. What a fascination this can be! A nestbox situated close to the house offers you the privilege and the opportunity to share in the everyday life of the tit family. You can watch the house hunting, the feverish nest-building, the difficulty the female has to squeeze in the hole as she becomes plump with an egg – and then endure with her the comparatively dull fortnight of incubation.

Once the young hatch, life becomes hectic again. Garden broods tend to be of eight to ten young, woodland up to fifteen or even

more! Fortunately for the parents, feeding them non-stop for about three weeks, there is normally only one brood each season. You can gauge the rigours: before she lays, the female will increase in weight by up to 50% in a fortnight, but all of this increase, and more, is worn away by the hundreds of food-carrying trips made each day by the parents trying to satisfy the demands of apparently bottom-less youngsters.

HERRING GULL

If sheer increase in numbers is an indication of success, then Herring Gulls – currently expanding their population at a phenomenal 10% per annum – are clearly extremely successful birds. The majority breed on rocky coasts where the cliffs are sufficiently towering to be undisturbed by man. In the north and west, in the absence of man, they will breed on low rocky islets and sand dunes. Usually pairs are widely scattered, not in the typically dense concentration of a gull colony, but as numbers increase in areas where suitable colony sites are scarce – like the Bristol Channel – huge and dense gulleries are forming. This expansion is putting considerable pressure on other coastal birds, desiring to nest in the same habitat but lacking the Herring Gull's size, power and aggression. Many tern colonies, in particular, are threatened in this way, and finding an effective and acceptable technique to stem the advance of the gulls is a serious problem in many coastal nature reserves.

There are now a number of inland colonies in remote moorland areas, and many instances of Herring Gulls breeding on rooftops in coastal towns. This habit started in Dover in the 1920s, and has spread rapidly. The raucous 'dawn chorus' of Herring Gulls, which starts in the early hours of the morning, and liberal aerial bombardment of unsuspecting holidaymakers with droppings has led to a sharp fall in the 'popularity' of the 'seagull'.

It is strange to think that at the turn of the century, gulls were rare birds inland – hence the term 'seagull' – and indeed only ventured inland in stormy weather. Today it would be difficult to spend a day anywhere in Britain without seeing numbers of several gull species, and the sight of straggling V-formations heading for the coast or a nearby lake or reservoir is commonplace towards dark. What is the reason for this change? Probably that gulls exhibit great versatility in feeding, which has led to changes in distribution. The smaller gulls – Common and Black-headed – exploit the opportunities offered by farming: following the plough and eating worms is a good example. But all the gulls exploit refuse – the visible and, to them, edible evidence of man's increasing affluence and living standards during this century. In winter, no town rubbish tip is likely to be without a scrabbling mass of gulls turning over the refuse in search of food. Gulls' standards of hygiene differ from ours, and the proximity of tips to reservoirs suitable for bathing and

roosting gives rise to concern for public health.

Many Herring Gull nests allow easy watching for holidaymakers of some of the intricacies of bird behaviour. Sit at a distance, to avoid disturbance, and watch through binoculars. Perhaps the neatest aspect is the soliciting of food by the speckled grey youngsters. They have plaintive wheedling cries, but no matter how persistently uttered, these are of no avail until the chick pecks at the red spot, clearly visible at the tip of the adults' yellow beak. This stimulus releases the feeding response, and the adult disgorges a meal. On the face of it, birds seem to have ridiculously-stereotyped behaviour patterns, but clearly they lead to success.

NUTHATCH

On superficial inspection, you could be forgiven for thinking that the Nuthatch was a sort of small woodpecker, so similar are its movements on a tree trunk. But notice that the Nuthatch scrambles about just as easily head-down as head-up. Unlike the woodpecker family, which have specially strong central tail feathers that they use almost as a shooting-stick – a prop to support them on the bark that only functions when they are head-uppermost, Nuthatches have a soft tail, and can move in any direction.

They occur most commonly in mature or aged deciduous woodland, particularly favouring areas where beech, oak and sweet chestnut occur to provide winter food. Open parkland and in many parts, large gardens with decrepit trees also appear attractive to them, but their distribution over Britain is erratic and often puzzling, as many apparently suitable areas have no Nuthatches!

Dove-grey above, rich chestnut on the flanks fading to fawn on the belly, with a large effective-looking beak and a striking black patch through the eye, Nuthatches are very attractive birds. They are sparrow-sized, and the male has conspicuously larger and darker chestnut patches on his flanks than the female. Because of their attractiveness, there have been attempts to introduce them to Scotland and Ireland (where they are totally absent) but these have not proved successful.

Although they do take insects and their larvae, particularly in summer, Nuthatches specialise on nuts. Larger and harder ones, like chestnuts, beechmast and hazel nuts are carried in the beak to a suitable (and regularly used) crevice in the bark or masonry of a nearby building and hammered open with the beak. This characteristic hammering is one of the best ways of locating them in winter. In many areas, Nuthatches are regular and popular visitors to the garden bird table, where they eat most offerings including fat. Often they will take away tougher items like peanuts (or even hard toast) and subject them to the anvil treatment on their favourite trunk.

In early spring, Nuthatches are very noisy, their ringing monosyllabic calls and trilling song being far-carrying. The elaborate, but usually concealed black-and-white patterns beneath the tail and under the wings are used during the short display season, and once nesting is under way the birds are quiet and secretive. They nest in

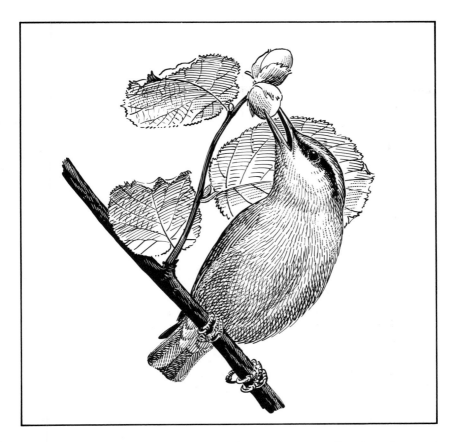

holes or cavities, often far larger than necessary, flooring the nest
chamber, very characteristically, with flakes of dry bark. Another
character of all Nuthatches' nests, even those in nestboxes, is the
liberal plastering of mud that seems part of the essential pattern of
Nuthatch life. A nestbox lid may be cemented firmly on in this way,
and over-sized entrance holes are plastered round inside to reduce
them to the correct diameter. They may use astonishing quantities
of mud: in Sussex some nests in cavities in ricks had several pounds
of mud to reinforce the fragile entrance!

GREAT SPOTTED WOODPECKER

Although far less colourful than the Green Woodpecker, in no way could the predominately black-and-white Great Spotted Woodpecker be called drab. Rather larger than a Song Thrush, it is elegantly black, with white spots above, and white below, with a big patch of red under the tail and a patch of red on the nape of the male. They have a sharp call, but far more often draw attention to themselves in spring and summer by brief bursts of drumming, akin to the timbre of a kettle drum.

Drumming is usually concerned with territory. For many years the noise was thought to be made vocally, but now we know that the male chooses a series of prominant perches – often dead branches – with suitable resonating properties, and hammers on them with its beak to proclaim its territorial boundaries. Why they do not suffer from splitting headaches remains something of a mystery, but perhaps part of their salvation lies in a cushion of shock-absorbing tissue between beak and skull. They use the beak as both hammer and chisel to excavate a nest hole, and to dig insects out of bark or timber. They eat nuts, too, but the tapping as they break into a hazel nut, held in the natural vice of a crevice in the bark, is much slower and more deliberate, quite different from drumming.

Great Spotted Woodpeckers are versatile feeders, not averse to snatching the odd tit nestling from its hole and devouring it. In winter, they are fast becoming regular visitors to garden bird-tables, and are specially fond of nuts and suet. They will even, on occasion, chop through the suspending string to drop a tempting morsel to the ground where they, too, can get at it!

As the breeding season gets underway, the Great Spotted Woodpeckers become more vocal, and sometimes indulge in excited chases round and round tree trunks, with much puppy-like 'chacking' as they go. We always see woodpeckers head-up on trees. Besides a specialist beak and tongue, they have powerful toes set (unusually for birds) two forward, two back, to give the best grip on a vertical tree. They also have specially strong tail feathers, which they use as a prop: rather like a shooting-stick or the third leg of a tripod. The tongue is long, but instead of being sticky, like the Green Woodpeckers, it is armed with a pointed and barbed horny tip, like a harpoon. Having chipped through the bark, the woodpecker stabs the luckless insect larva it has found with its barbed

tongue, probing for some distance along the insect's tunnel if necessary.

The same goes for our remaining woodpecker, the Lesser Spotted. Barred black and white above, it lacks the red beneath the tail of the Greater, and at about sparrow-size, it is conspicuously smaller than its relative. Dutch elm disease has ravaged our countryside, but it is good to know that at least one family of birds has benefited from all the dead timber left lying to rot after the disease has done its work. Benefit the woodpeckers certainly have, to the extent that the once scarce Lesser Spotted is now widespread, and most of us should be able to hear it drumming, higher pitched and in longer bursts than the Great Spotted. Late in the summer it will be taking yet another advantage of dead trees, sending its drumming across a woodland, quieter now that the breeding season is coming to a close.

WILD GEESE

Few birdwatching sights or sounds are more evocative, or more wildly beautiful, than skeins of geese flying across a wintry sky. Apart from the Canada Goose – large and black-necked, with a white 'chin-strap' – that was introduced from North America in the reign of King Charles and is now widely established as a resident on park lakes and gravel pits, our geese are mostly migrants, breeding on the Arctic tundra. Some breed on remote islands with fascinating names from the age of polar exploration: Spitzbergen, Novaya Zemlya and Franz Josef Land.

Broadly speaking, there are two types of geese: grey, and black. Two species of black geese occur regularly: the Barnacle Goose, with a white face and silver flanks, is a bird of coastal grassland in the north and west; and the Brent Goose, almost all-black and a bird of sheltered estuary mudflats. Here it seeks its specialist food, the eelgrass *Zostera*. Recently, Brent Goose numbers have increased rapidly, following a population crash when *Zostera* was almost eliminated by disease. As a result, the geese are turning to winter-sown cereals planted on newly-drained marshland adjacent to the estuaries, and are causing some concern to farmers.

Largest of the grey geese is the Greylag, ancestor of many domestic geese. Its large size, pale grey forewings and cackling call reminiscent of the farmyard make it easy to identify. Greylags are numerous and widespread in Scotland, and a small population of truly wild birds breeds in the Outer Hebrides. Elsewhere in Britain, groups of Greylags, artificially introduced, often by wildfowling clubs, now breed freely.

Often to be seen with Greylags on stubble, or gleaning the leftovers of the potato harvest, is the smallest of the grey geese, the Pink-footed Goose. The very dark neck and small stubby beak are the best identification features. They, too, are common in Scotland, becoming scarcer the further south you travel. The common goose of southern Britain is the White-fronted, easily recognised by the white face patch and dark bars on the breast of the adults. Geese are noisy birds, and a flock of White-fronts in flight produces a continuous yelping laughter-like babble. Ringing recoveries show that English birds originate in Russia, while those on the west coast of Scotland and Ireland are a separate race breeding in Greenland. White-fronts love short turf, and often move on to winter wheat,

where usually their grazing increases the number of shoots (tillers) on the plant to the benefit of the crop.

Geese usually fly in a staggered 'V' formation, often with several side branches. Aerodynamic research indicates that there may be a good purpose in this. Not only can older, experienced and more powerful birds (usually females) take turns in leading and navigating, but the birds in the arms of the V each derive some benefit, in the form of additional 'lift', from the turbulence created by the beating wings of the birds in front. In this way, the group of family parties has the best chance of both remaining on course and of conserving energy on a long and hazardous migration journey.

ROBIN

The Robin was voted our national bird some years ago – deservedly so, as its popularity extends from the garden to the cards on the mantelpiece at Christmas. At the turn of the century, the old English 'Robin Redbreast' was abbreviated to just 'Redbreast' as the commonly-used name, but this has now been superseded by the more popular contraction 'Robin'.

Robins have always been at the centre of superstition, and to kill one was regarded almost as sacrilege: a feeling perpetuated even now in the nursery rhyme 'Who killed Cock Robin?' These beliefs, and the Robin's popularity as a Christmas feature, stem from the legend that the Robin attempted to draw the nails (or, alternatively, remove the crown of thorns) at the crucifixion, receiving for its efforts a drop of Christ's blood, and ever after bore a red bib.

Beneath a friendly exterior, the Robin is a tough little customer. The two sexes are alike in plumage, and even Robins only seem able to tell who's who on the basis of behaviour. In winter, male and female set up separate feeding territories (although there may sometimes be common ground around the bird table), and she will hold her own just as well as he, hurling abuse at any invader and chasing it off. As spring advances, under the influence of hormonal changes induced by warmer weather and longer days, her attitude softens. She ceases to sing at the same time as hormonal changes in the male cause his song to become fuller and richer in tone. He also becomes more aggressive, and seeks to expand his territorial boundaries: she, instead of reacting violently as in the past, acquiesces submissively.

Her passive reaction to his aggression leads to a change in his behaviour, he gradually accepts her presence and a pair bond is formed. From then on, he will defend the territory, while she feeds furiously to build herself up for the rigours of the breeding season. Her mate will help, in a charming manner, by offering her extra and juicy food items. This gesture is called 'courtship feeding', and was thought to cement the pair bond in the same way that flowers or chocolates do in human relationships. More pragmatic modern theory suggests that she will come into breeding condition sooner with this assistance, thus increasing the chances of a successful breeding season.

The Robin's tameness in the garden, sitting on the fork handle or

darting almost beneath the prongs to retrieve a freshly-uncovered worm during the winter digging can only add to its popularity. So, too, must its habit of singing in winter as well as in summer. The winter song is more fragile, and higher pitched than the summer version, reaching across the garden like a thread of gossamer glistening in the sun: as much a part of autumn and winter as bonfire smoke.